monetary theory

inflation, interest,
and growth
in the world economy

Robert A. Mundell
University of Chicago

 Goodyear Publishing Company, Inc.
Pacific Palisades, California

© 1971
by GOODYEAR PUBLISHING COMPANY, INC.
Pacific Palisades, California

Current printing (last digit) :

10 9 8 7 6 5 4 3 2 1

Y5864–7

ISBN: 0–87620–586–4

Library of Congress Catalog Card No. : 74–123615

Printed in the United States of America

to my father

contents

II THE WORLD ECONOMY

acknowledgments

I am indebted to many sources for ideas, techniques, and perspectives in the field of monetary theory. The writings of Irving Fisher, Frank Knight, John Maynard Keynes, and Paul Samuelson represent the major early influences. In the 1950's, the works of Lloyd Metzler, Don Patinkin, Milton Friedman, and James Tobin stand out. In the 1960's, the interaction (especially with Chicago friends) is too complex to record in detail and is noted where possible in the book. I should like to mention, however, Miguel Sidrauski, whose untimely death robbed the profession of a precocious intellect.

I should like to thank D. Purvis, R. Dornbusch, J. Frenkel, and Babu Jones for their help in the preparation of the final manuscript.

monetary theory

introduction

Keynes' *General Theory* was written in the 1930s. Its premises reflect the uncertainties of that decade. Keynes assumed rigid wages, no growth, a closed economy, and exogenous expectations. The Keynesian model is a *short run* model of a *closed* economy, dominated by *pessimistic* expectations and *rigid* wages. This model is not relevant to modern economies.

Keynes was acutely aware of the importance of expectations in linking the present and future. He rejected the notion that expectations could be embodied in any mechanical hypothesis relating the present and future. Ironically, this agnostic attitude, attributable to the importance he attached to the role of expectations, was transmogrified in the mathematized versions of the Keynesian model into the most mechanical and naive of all expectations hypotheses: that the future will be like the present. In a world conditioned to progress this amounts to a very pessimistic view of the future.

From 1940 to the present the world economy experienced the greatest sustained period of growth in history, creating an economic environment and a psychological orientation exactly opposite to that in which Keynes wrote. This environmental change has rendered the expectations premises of the *General Theory* obsolete. The stagnation-pessimism orientation of the closed Keynesian depression model cannot be sustained in a growing world economy experiencing secular inflation and rapid growth.

There is, however, a lack of alternatives to the Keynesian system in the literature.

This book attempts to provide one. Its basic conception is a growing world economy composed of interacting national economies. It takes the eighteenth century Humean conception of an interdependent world monetary system and incorporates into it Keynes' analytical developments, modifying his premises and synthesizing his results with the modern theory of economic growth. Its primary aim is to find an inflationary complement to the Keynesian depression model. Keynes' theory attempts to explain unemployment equilibrium; this book focuses on inflationary equilibrium. The two models come together at full employment and stable prices. Except at this boundary case, the premises of the two models are different.

In place of the Keynesian expectations assumptions this book assumes that if spot prices rise they will maintain their new level or, in an inflationary environment, go on rising. In states of rapid inflation or hyperinflation, expected inflation rates may even accelerate. Growth and the balance of payments are also explicitly introduced into the analysis. The only closed economy is the world economy.

The ideas developed in this book matured at different stages back in the 1950s and 1960s, and some of them are part of the literature of the period. The first half of the book presents the analytical infrastructure underlying the world system presented in the second half. The object is to combine the essential features of the specific models of Hume, Fisher, and Keynes in a more general theory of interest, inflation, and growth of the world economy. I do not claim to have resolved all the problems associated with a new approach, but only to have helped build, with able predecessors and contemporaries, a better foundation for modern monetary theory.

new ideas in monetary theory

chapter 1

money, debt,
and the
rate of interest

We begin by analyzing the effects of nonrecurrent changes in the quantity of money and the public debt on the price level and the rate of interest. This chapter compares differences that arise when changes in the money supply are brought about simply or along with changes in the public debt (open market operations). It shows that the primary significance of the public debt lies in its effect on the capitalization of future income streams. It raises the problem of the optimum debt-income ratio of an economy and the optimal distribution of total debt between the government and the public.

The analysis is relevant to both stabilization policy and debt policy. In the inter run it makes no difference to the equilibrium price level whether increases in the money supply are brought about by simple increases in the money supply or by open market operations, except insofar as it changes the debt-income ratio of the economy. When government debt is in the form of nonindexed bonds inflation lowers the debt-income ratio in the short run and its distribution between the public and private issuers in the inter run and thus imparts a nonneutrality dimension to simple monetary expansion in the short run. In the inter run and long

Adapted from "The Public Debt, Corporate Income Taxes and the Rate of Interest," *Journal of Political Economy* 68 (Dec. 1960): 622–26, by permission of The University of Chicago Press. Copyright 1961 by the University of Chicago.

run the implication is that the absence of a public debt would leave the economy undercapitalized.

THE ECONOMIC SYSTEM

To abstract from distributional considerations arising from changes in the price level, we assume that government interest payments are fixed in *real* terms and that the monetary values of corporate dividends rise and fall in proportion to the price level; this means that the aggregate real value of all securities will be approximately equal to the capitalized value of corporate dividends and government interest payments, the capitalization being done at the prevailing rate of interest. We also assume that wages and prices are flexible, that the supply of labor is inelastic, and that full employment is continuously maintained.

The economic system can be in equilibrium only if the capital and goods (and services) markets are in balance. The capital market is in balance when the community wishes to hold the existing stock of securities, and the goods market is in equilibrium when real saving equals real investment.

Mathematically, the system can be described by the following equations:

$$S(r, m, A) = I(r) \tag{1}$$

which states that saving must equal investment if the goods market is to be in equilibrium; and

$$A = B(r,m) \tag{2}$$

which is the equilibrium in the capital market, where r is the interest rate, m is real balances, A is the value of assets, B is the demand for assets, S is saving, and I is investment. The definition of assets is

$$A = \frac{D}{r} + \frac{G}{r} \tag{3}$$

where D and G are, respectively, the real values of dividends and government interest payments, assumed constant in the absence of open-market operations and tax changes. The partial derivatives, $\partial S/\partial m$, $\partial S/\partial A$, and $\partial S/\partial(m + A)$ can be referred to, respectively, as the real balance effect, the asset effect, and the wealth effect, and are all assumed to be negative.

A geometric interpretation of the system can be developed by using equation (3) to eliminate A from equations (1) and (2). The resulting equations are represented by the IS and AB schedules in Figure 1-1.

The AB schedule traces the locus of pairs of interest rates and real cash balances which are compatible with equilibrium in the capital market:

this curve has a negative slope because both an increase in the rate of interest and an increase in real balances increase the demand for securities relative to the supply of securities. The *IS* schedule, on the other hand, expresses the relation between rates of interest and levels of real balances along which the goods market is in equilibrium: this curve has a positive slope because an increase in the rate of interest is deflationary, while an increase in real balances is inflationary.

The system is in general equilibrium at the point Q, common to both schedules. Under the usual dynamic postulates, this point is a *stable* equilibrium: any departure of the system from the equilibrium values

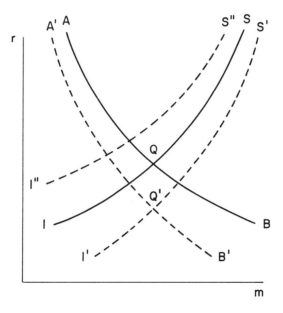

Figure 1-1   The rate of interest is plotted on the ordinate and the level of real cash balances on the abscissa. *IS* and *AB* are the initial schedules showing the loci of interest rates and real balances which permit equilibrium in, respectively, the goods and capital markets. After the open-market operation the new schedules are *I'S'* and *A'B'* on the assumption that the capital market is imperfect and that income taxes are reduced. If corporate taxes are reduced, the *IS* schedule shifts to *I"S"* after the open-market operation, while the *AB* schedule is unaltered. If the capital market is perfect, the open-market purchase combined with a reduction in income taxes does not shift the schedules.

represented by Q will set in motion dynamic forces inducing a return to equilibrium. Our concern, however, is not with the dynamic operation of the system, but rather in the effect of changes in the quantity of money and the public debt on the equilibrium itself.

THE QUANTITY OF MONEY AND
THE RATE OF INTEREST

It is easily demonstrated that a simple change in the nominal quantity of money has no effect on the real equilibrium of the system. From Q, the initial equilibrium, an increase in the money supply would temporarily move the level of real balances to the right of Q, but dynamic forces operating in the capital and goods markets would then induce changes in the price level which would restore the original level of *real* cash balances. After the change in the money supply, the nominal values of wages, prices, taxes, and assets would have changed in the same proportion as the money supply, but the rate of interest would be unaltered.

Mathematically, the system can be completed by the equation

$$m = \frac{M}{P} \tag{4}$$

where P is the price level and M is the nominal quantity of money, assumed to be determined by the central bank. It is readily seen that the equilibrium of the reduced system

$$S\left(r, \frac{M}{P}, \frac{D+G}{r}\right) = I(r) \tag{5}$$

$$\frac{D+G}{r} = B\left(r, \frac{M}{P}\right) \tag{6}$$

depends only on the ratio M/P and not on the nominal level of M.

This result can be used in our analysis of open-market operations. An open-market operation involves an exchange of money and government securities between the central bank (or government) and the public. But, since the money component of this exchange does not affect the final equilibrium, open-market operations can be analyzed as a simple change in outstanding government debt.

THE PUBLIC DEBT AND THE RATE
OF INTEREST

If the central bank buys government securities (with newly created money), the government no longer pays interest on these securities; the government debt is reduced, and so is the government interest bill. In the absence of other changes, then, the government would experience a budget surplus and the public a reduction in disposable income equal to the reduced interest payments. To abstract from this disequilibrium situation, I assume that the government reduces taxes, as a result of the open-market operations, by an amount equal to the reduced interest payments, thus maintaining a balanced budget.

The method by which taxes are reduced is crucial to the final result. If income taxes are reduced and the capital market is not so perfect that it can discount any certain income stream, the rate of interest is lowered by open-market purchases. But if corporation taxes are lowered, the rate of interest rises.

To prove these propositions it is sufficient to show how the two schedules shift as a result of the open-market purchases and the tax reductions. Suppose, first, that income taxes are lowered. At constant interest rates the real value of earning assets is reduced, and this affects both the capital and the goods markets. In the capital market there is excess demand for securities at the same rate of interest and level of real balances, which means that balance can be restored only at a lower level of real balances or at a lower rate of interest; in other words, the AB schedule shifts west at any given rate of interest, or south at any given level of real balances, to a new position such as $A'B'$. In the goods market, on the other hand, there is excess supply because the lower level of earning assets induces the public to augment their wealth by greater saving. Only at a higher level of real balances or a lower rate of interest, then, can equilibrium in the goods market be restored; the IS schedule thus shifts south and east to a new position, such as $I'S'$. But if AB shifts west and IS shifts east, the new intersection Q' implies a lower equilibrium rate of interest. Open-market purchases combined with income tax reductions therefore lower the equilibrium rate of interest.[1]

Now consider the case where corporate income taxes are lowered. At constant interest rates the number of securities held by the community is reduced, but the total value of securities remains unchanged—the values of corporates rise to compensate for the fall in the aggregate values of governments. Initially, the open-market purchase reduces the value of securities, but when the interest payments on the securities bought are handed over to corporations in the form of reduced corporate taxes and then redistributed to stockholders as dividends, assuming no change in retained profits, the value of corporate securities rises. If, for instance, the central bank managed to buy one-quarter of the available securities in the economy, the value of securities would be initially reduced by one-

---

1. See Metzler's treatment of this case in "Wealth, Saving and the Rate of Interest," *Journal of Political Economy* 59 (Apr. 1951): 93–116.

quarter at a constant interest rate; but the reduction in corporate income taxes would be responsible for an increase in the value of remaining securities by one-third. Wealth does not change, so the AB schedule does not shift.

More formally this result can be demonstrated in the context of the model by showing the relation between taxes and government interest payments.

Let y_0 be full-employment output, z, a constant, the share of profits, and t^* the rate at which corporate income is taxed, expressed as a fraction. Then dividends, D, are equal to $zy_0(1 - t^*)$, and government interest payments, G, are equal to zy_0t^* if they are financed by corporate taxes. The real value of aggregate assets then equals

$$A = \frac{D}{r} + \frac{G}{r} = \frac{zy_0(1 - t^*)}{r} + \frac{zy_0t^*}{r} = \frac{zy_0}{r}.$$

Thus a change in government interest payments financed or disposed of by a change in corporate taxes does not affect the aggregate value of corporate and government securities.

The practical question of whether a change in the public debt affects the equilibrium rate of interest cannot, however, stop at this point, for we have not yet taken account of possible shifts in the IS schedule due to a change in investment. Corporate income taxes constitute a tax on capital and have allocation effects. Because of the reduction in corporate income taxes, the spread between what capital produces and what savers receive is reduced. Business firms will therefore find that previously unattractive investments have become worth undertaking because the real productivity of capital is unchanged, while, in the absence of new issues, corporate securities have risen in price. Investment thus increases, and the IS schedule shifts to the left, to, say, $I''S''$, inducing a higher rate of interest. Open-market purchases combined with corporate income tax reductions therefore *raise* the equilibrium rate of interest.

ECONOMIC EXPLANATION

The manner by which taxes are changed in conjunction with open-market operations is of crucial importance to the final effect on the rate of interest: if income taxes are lowered, the rate of interest falls; but if corporate taxes are lowered, the rate of interest rises. The reason lies in a comparison of the roles of changes in the money supply and in the government debt. Money is the government's *noninterest-bearing* debt, and changes in it do not affect any real values at the final equilibrium. Thus they cannot affect the rate of interest, abstracting from changes in the distribution of income, "menu costs," or transitory effects on resource allocation. But changes in the government's *interest-bearing* debt necessitate an adjustment of taxes if budget balance is preserved, and these tax changes are almost certain to alter the level of disposable income, the distribution of income, the allocation of resources, or the extent to which income streams are capitalized in the securities market.

This insight places in a wider perspective the results obtained in the preceding section. Since we have abstracted throughout this chapter from changes in the distribution and level of income, the previous statement implies that changes in the government debt can affect the rate of interest only if the allocation of resources is changed or if the capital market contains imperfections. This is, in fact, the explanation of the changes in the rate of interest after open-market operations. When open-market purchases are combined with a reduction in corporate taxes, the negative wealth effect of the reduction in the public debt is cancelled by the positive wealth effect of the capital gains experienced by owners of corporate securities. There is no net wealth effect so that any change in the rate of interest can only arise from an allocation effect; the shift from government debt to corporate debt will not be fully offset by new corporate issues and therefore will lower the rate of interest. The rate of interest falls, on the other hand, when open-market purchases are combined with income tax reductions because capitalizable government interest payments are converted into noncapitalizable tax reductions; if the capital market were perfect, all income streams including tax reductions could be bought and sold, and the rate of interest would be unaltered. In neither case is it correct to attribute the change in the rate of interest to the wealth effect on saving.

In the real world some expected income streams are not readily capitalizable because of information costs, transactions costs, and various risks. An argument for the public debt can be made in pure theory on the grounds of narrowing a gap between the marginal private cost and the marginal social cost of capitalization. But the neutrality of the public debt cannot be discussed outside the context of the taxes used to service it. All taxes have income effects, and the issue of neutrality of the public debt, leaving aside allocation and distribution effects, is whether the income effects are capitalizable into wealth effects. The corporate income tax offers an example of a capitalizable tax and a case where a decrease in the public debt accompanied by a reduction in corporate taxes equal to the reduced real interest payments of the government leaves wealth unchanged except insofar as credit ratings of the government and the corporations are different; both are, or are usually taken to be, unperishable institutions. Individuals, however, except for members of credit-worthy dynastic families, cannot capitalize fully future tax payments so that a net wealth effect is likely to be operative.

We may conclude by noting the effect of the assumption that securities are entirely in the form of equities or indexed securities. To the extent that the public debt is in the form of bonds the propositions are in the main unchanged except insofar as liquidity effects alter the price level. An increase in the nominal quantity of money, for example, will raise the price level and lower the real value of the public debt and consequently the real burden of the taxes needed to finance interest on the debt.[2] If taxes are fixed in real terms the government will experience a surplus and reduce taxes, which again will be capitalized to a degree that will depend on the type of tax and the perfectness of the capital market; whereas if taxes are fixed in nominal terms the real burden of taxes will again be lowered and the same principles regarding the degree of capitalization apply. In all cases it is the degree of capitalization, apart from allocative and redistributive effects of the tax changes, that determines the impact on the rate of interest. The conclusions can be enriched by noting the dynamic effects of open-market operations when the budget is left un-balanced, leading to speculative effects and capital gains of the type considered in subsequent chapters.

It is necessary, however, to conclude with a qualification that can be of some practical significance. The equilibrium rate of interest considered throughout this chapter is a "growth equilibrium" rate intermediate between that which equilibrates the capital market, but does not take account of the equilibrium conditions in the goods market, and that which obtains when the capital stock is in equilibrium (the "thoroughgoing" equilibrium rate of the stationary state). The system depicted in the diagram does not take account of the growing capital stock and its effect on output and the marginal product of capital, nor does it allow for the gradual accumulation of assets represented by the offerings of new securities to finance current investment. This, however, is not a limitation, since any proof that a change in the public debt does or does not affect the rate of interest implies a proof that a change can or cannot affect the equilibrium configuration at the stationary state.

CONCLUSIONS

A change in the quantity of money alters the price level but leaves the rate of interest unaltered, except for some qualifications to be noted. A change in the money supply accompanied by a change in the public

---

2. Keynes was aware of this point, noting that ". . . the effect of the lower price level on the real burden of the National Debt and hence on taxation is likely to prove very adverse to business confidence." *The General Theory of Employment, Interest and Money* (London: Macmillan Co., 1961), p. 264.

debt (open market operations) *appears* to affect the level of wealth and would thus affect saving and the rate of interest. However, this ignores the offsetting effect on *wealth* of the *capitalized value* of future tax liabilities used to finance the interest on the debt. If the private economy can completely capitalize these liabilities there will be no change in wealth, and open market operations will have the same effect on prices and interest as a simple equal change in the quantity of money. The significance of the public debt thus lies in its effect on the public capitalization of the economy.

The optimum level of the public debt is that which equates the marginal social cost of public capitalization of income streams with the marginal social benefits of capitalization. The social benefits of public capitalization will exceed costs if the private economy is undercapitalized, as it probably is due to the imperfect capitalization of human income. An optimum expansion of money will reduce the capitalization of the economy and thus lower the rate of interest if the public debt is in the form of bonds. Thus a simple monetary expansion would lower the degree of capitalization except insofar as the private economy is able to capitalize the gain in expected disposable income due to the lower real value of expected tax payments. But open market operations aggravate the undercapitalization which, again from an optimum, results from simple monetary expansion. The public debt can thus be looked on as a means by which the government can correct any distortion due to undercapitalization of the private economy. The *optimum* public debt will vary with the size of the economy and the private institutional costs of internalizing the externalities of a decentralized capital market, which in some societies could even be negative.

Certain optimality properties associated with money holdings can also be considered. When trust in public money rests not on its intrinsic value—as in the case of metals under free coinage systems—but on faith in government credit, the central bank can maintain securities as backing for its fiduciary issue. The income from these securities—leaving aside real expenses of printing and distributing fiat money—creates a negative rate of monetary expansion and leads to deflation and a theorem on optimum money holdings: that money should earn a rate of return such that the marginal social benefit of hoards is equal to the marginal social cost.

In calculating social benefits and costs, however, it is necessary to recognize the frictions of transactions costs in a state of barter and the role of money as a medium of exchange in reducing these costs of transactions. A similar caveat is necessary to take into account the role of money in reducing information costs insofar as money serves as a unit of account and contract. These properties of money are of the utmost importance in the real world, even though they have not been adequately assimilated into technical economic theory.

chapter 2

inflation, saving, and the real rate of interest

Whereas the previous chapter dealt with *nonrecurrent* injections of money or government debt into the economic system, this chapter examines the impact of *repetitive* injections of money on the price level and the rate of interest. Whereas before we could assume that the public did not foresee the consequences for the future price level, we now have to take adjustments in expectations of inflation into account.

This chapter's theoretical contribution lies in its integration of three previously unconnected parts of the literature: Fisher's theory of appreciation and interest, Keynes' theory of liquidity preference, and Pigou's theory of wealth and saving. For this purpose it develops a diagrammatic analysis introduced into the literature by Lloyd Metzler in a famous paper written in 1950. This synthesis demonstrates that inflation increases saving and lowers the real rate of interest so that the money rate of interest rises by less than the rate of inflation. It thus provides an alternative explanation of the paradox discovered by Fisher and attributed by him to money illusions and imperfect adaptation of expectations.

The implication of the argument is that monetary expansion can

Adapted from "Inflation and Real Interest," *Journal of Political Economy* 71 (June 1963): 280–83, by permission of The University of Chicago Press. Copyright 1963 by the University of Chicago.

alter the intertemporal distribution of income and the equilibrium capital stock, even when the inflation is fully anticipated.

INADEQUACIES OF FISHER'S THEORY

Irving Fisher's analysis of the interest rate under inflation, which concluded that the money rate of interest rises by the anticipated rate of inflation or falls by the anticipated rate of deflation, was subjected to attack by Keynes: "The mistake lies in supposing that it is the rate of interest on which prospective changes in the value of money will directly react, instead of the marginal efficiency of a given stock of capital."[1] Fisher himself seems to have had misgivings about the *empirical* reliability of his explanation and presented evidence suggesting that the adjustment of money interest was only partial, concluding:

> When the cost of living is not stable, the rate of interest takes the appreciation and depreciation into account to some extent, but only slightly, and, in general, indirectly. That is, when prices are rising, the rate of interest tends to be high but not so high as it should be to compensate for the rise; and when prices are falling, the rate of interest tends to be low, but not so low as it should be to compensate for the fall.[2]

Later he showed that the real rate of interest was much more variable than the money rate and conjectured that

> Men are unable or unwilling to adjust at all accurately and promptly the money interest rates to changed price levels.... The erratic behavior of real interest is evidently a trick played on the money market by the "money illusion" when contracts are made in unstable money.[3]

Thus Fisher found verification for a theory of *partial* adjustment of money interest to inflation and deflation but none for his own theory of *complete* adjustment under foresight. And to attribute the discrepancy between theory and reality solely to lack of foresight is to raise doubts about the nature of the evidence that would be required to reject the theory.

The theory presented in this chapter is more consistent with Fisher's empirical observations than his own theory, for it shows that anticipated inflation or deflation is likely to raise (lower) the money rate of interest by less than the rate of inflation (deflation) itself. It is also consistent with

1. J. M. Keynes, *The General Theory of Employment, Interest and Money* (London: Macmillan Co., 1961) p. 143.
2. *The Theory of Interest* (New York: Macmillan Co., 1930), p. 43.
3. *Ibid.*, p. 415.

Keynes' theoretical criticism of Fisher, yet paradoxically retains the concept of an equilibrium interest rate uninfluenced by unanticipated once-for-all changes in the quantity of money.

INFLATION AND THE DISCREPANCY BETWEEN REAL AND MONEY INTEREST RATES

To analyze the problem we shall utilize the apparatus invented by Lloyd Metzler in his celebrated article, "Wealth, Saving, and the Rate of Interest."[4] It is assumed that wages and prices are flexible, that full employment is continuously maintained, and that the share of profits in full employment income is constant. Wealth is assumed to be held in money and shares, the real value of the latter being real profits capitalized at the going real interest rate. It is further assumed that real investment depends on the real interest rate and real saving on real balances and that wealth-holders divide their assets between money and securities in a proportion which depends on the money rate of interest.

Under these conditions the equilibrium interest rate is determined by the intersection of two schedules, in some respect analogous to the Hicksian *LM* and *IS* curves (see Figure 2-1). The *IS* schedule plots the locus of pairs of values of real interest rates and real money balances along which saving is equal to investment. Its slope is positive because an increase in the real interest rate lowers investment, causing a deflationary gap, while an increase in real balances lowers saving, causing a compensating inflationary gap. Thus, an increase in the real interest rate would have to be associated with an increase in real balances[5] in order to maintain equality between real saving and real investment. Points above and to the left of

4. *Journal of Political Economy* 59 (April 1951): 93–116.
5. Wealth changes along *IS* by less than the change in real money balances since the real value of equities moves in inverse proportion to the real rate of interest; the *wealth* effect along *IS* is therefore less than the *real balance* effect, though it is still in the same direction.

It is easy to allow a certain carelessness of language to perpetuate a confusion between two things: the effect on wealth or on the real value of money balances of a decrease in the price level, and the *effect on spending* occasioned by such an increase in real balances. The "wealth effect" and the "real balance effect" refer only to the latter.

A further point of clarification is worth making. A reduction in the price level, for a given level of nominal money balances, has both a wealth effect and a substitution effect; the latter arises because the proportion of real liquidity in wealth increases. Thus, even if all money were "inside money," a decrease in the price level would induce, via the substitution effect, an increase in spending on goods insofar as liquid and non-liquid assets are to some extent net complements. The attempt to demonstrate that the real balance effect is insignificant, therefore, cannot be based solely on an argument that outside money is a small component of wealth. It must also establish the empirical proposition that the substitution effect is negligible.

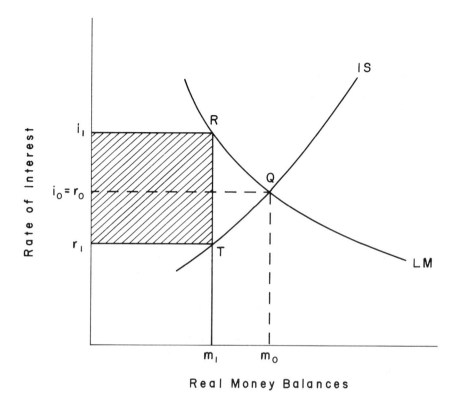

Figure 2-1

IS would be points of deflationary pressure and points below and to the right of *IS* would be points of inflationary pressure.

The *LM* schedule gives the locus of pairs of money interest rates and real money balances that is consistent with equilibrium in the money market. This schedule has a negative slope because asset-holders divide their wealth between money and securities in a proportion that depends on the opportunity cost of holding money, which is the *money* rate of interest. Thus at high money rates of interest the demand for real balances is low, and at low money interest rates the demand for real balances is high. Only along *LM* are people content to hold the existing stock of real money balances. Above *LM* there is excess liquidity and below *LM* there is deficient liquidity.

The *IS* and *LM* schedules intersect at *Q*, which determines the equilibrium interest rate, $r_0 = i_0$, and the equilibrium stock of real money balances, m_0. Only at *Q* is the desire to save equal to the incentive to invest, the demand for shares equal to the supply of shares, and the desire for real money balances equal to the existing stock of real money balances. *Q* is the equilibrium at which the price level is constant and, therefore, the equilibrium at which real and money interest rates are the same.[6]

THE FALL IN REAL INTEREST
UNDER INFLATION

Let us now consider the effects of anticipated inflation on the equilibrium. Inflation creates a discrepancy between money interest rates and real interest rates equal to the rate of inflation. This discrepancy widens the difference between the nominal earnings of shares and the return on money because the rate of depreciation of money (the inflation rate) must be added to the real return on shares to get the total cost of holding money.[7] Since the *LM* schedule is derived on the basis of a *money* rate of interest—as that measures the true cost of holding money—it follows that the *LM* schedule, as a function of the *real* rate of interest, shifts downward, at any given level of real balances, by the rate of the inflation. In Figure 2-1, for example, at the inflation rate RT the community would wish to hold the stock of real money balances m_1 only if the real interest rate were r_1 and the nominal interest rate were i_1, the difference being the rate of inflation RT. Thus, the entire schedule LM, which is fixed as a function of the *money* rate of interest, shifts downward, as a function of the *real* interest rate, by the rate of inflation.

Consider now the *IS* schedule. From any given point on the schedule an expected inflation, at a given nominal rate of interest, will create a divergence between the productivity of investment and the return on saving equal to the inflation rate, for a dollar borrowed at a given money rate of interest will yield a normal real return plus the rate of appreciation in value of goods, which corresponds to the rate of inflation itself. To maintain equality between saving and investment at any given rate of inflation, the nominal interest rate must therefore rise by the rate of inflation. In the figure, for example, the point T on the *IS* schedule gives a pair of values of real interest rates and real money balances at which saving is equal to investment at a zero rate of inflation. But if the expected inflation rate were RT, a *money* interest rate of only r_1 would create a discrepancy between investment and saving. Only if the nominal interest

---

6. This statement abstracts from economic growth, which is studied explicitly in the next chapter.

7. The following discussion of the demand for money under inflationary conditions has been helped by the works of Philip Cagan, "Monetary Dynamics of Hyperinflation," in *Studies in the Quantity Theory of Money*, ed. M. Friedman (Chicago: University of Chicago Press, 1956), pp. 25–117; and Martin Bailey, "Welfare Cost of Inflationary Finance," *Journal of Political Economy* 66 (1956): 93–110.

rate were increased to i_1 would investment and saving be equal at the level of real balances, m_1. The *IS* schedule therefore remains fixed, as a function of the *real* rate of interest, but is raised by the amount *RT*, as a function of the *money* rate of interest.

The ingredients of the solution are now established. If we interpret the ordinate of the figure as the *real* rate of interest it becomes necessary to shift the *LM* schedule downward by the anticipated rate of the inflation, while the *IS* curve is unaltered. If, on the other hand, the ordinate is taken to refer to the *money* rate of interest, the *IS* schedule must be shifted upward by the rate of the inflation, while the *LM* curve remains fixed. More simply, it is sufficient to take account of the discrepancy between the real rate of interest (for which the existing *IS* curve applies) and the money rate of interest (for which the existing *LM* schedule is appropriate), the discrepancy being the rate of the inflation.

The inflation itself is generated by monetary expansion *in excess of growth*. The rate of excess monetary expansion is equal to the rate of inflation, *RT*. The real rate of interest falls[8] from r_0 to r_1, while the money rate of interest rises from i_0 to i_1. Real money balances are reduced from m_0 to m_1 as a consequence of the shift in expectations, and real investment and real saving are both higher than in the inflationless equilibrium. The shaded area measures the depreciation of existing money balances.[9]

INTEREST-YIELDING MONEY

Subsequent to the 1963 publication of the above, Professor J. C. Weldon raised an interesting point that helps to focus attention on the nature of the "impurity" that separates the foregoing model from Fisher's. Weldon, in a private communication to the author in 1963, wrote:

8. The change in the rate of interest that results from the anticipation of inflation is a "permanent" change in the sense defined in my "Public Debt, Corporate Income Taxes and the Rate of Interest," *Journal of Political Economy* 68 (Dec. 1960): 625n. Recently Metzler's model has been subjected to further investigation, extension, and criticism (see George Horwich, "Real Assets and the Theory of Interest," *Journal of Political Economy* 70 [Apr. 1962]: 157–70; for references and a criticism of the monetary dynamics inherent in the system), but despite objections it seems to me that Metzler's system retains its essential utility, especially for "comparative statics" purposes.

9. If the new money issued were spent by the government on goods, the *IS* schedule would shift upward, whereas if it were spent on securities the *LM* schedule would shift downward; the rise in money interest will be greater than that shown in the diagram in the former case and smaller in the latter instance. The textual treatment has avoided these complications by postulating (implicitly) changes in the money supply unaccompanied by any physical quid pro quo to the government, a procedure that is probably justifiable for purposes of isolating the theoretical effects of pure inflation, even though it be lacking in institutional relevance.

"Mundell's specifications are met by a scheme, say, in which money consists of government notes, and in which it is universally known (or at least believed) that the government allows everyone to add an extra zero a year to the denominations of his notes (and similarly allows notes to be renumbered from time to time in proportion to growth). The anticipated inflation of 1,000 percent a year can have no real effects because all monetary calculations and contracts are naturally going to be determined de facto by the notes rather than their changing denominations. Fisher's theoretical finding should therefore be confirmed."

If moneyholders can upgrade their money as time passes, and if the rate at which the upgrading takes place is *identified* by moneyholders as a subsidy on real balances held, all real values of the variables will be unchanged. Weldon money is earning a pecuniary rate of interest equal to the rate of inflation of commodity prices. The cost of holding Weldon money is, therefore, not the real rate of interest plus the expected rate of inflation, but the real rate of interest plus the expected rate of inflation *minus* the pecuniary rate of interest on money itself. Since the latter, which is the rate at which "zeros are added," is *identified* with the expected rate of inflation, the cost of holding money is simply the real rate of interest. The *IS* and *LM* schedules remain fixed, as functions of the real rate of interest, and shift upward by the rate of inflation as functions of the nominal rate of interest.

This raises the important question as to the meaning of "price level" and "rate of inflation" when the monetary unit of account is itself undergoing transformation. A piece of Weldon money will always exchange for the same bundle of commodities, and the fact that we add zeros to the price of the commodity bundle at the same rate that we add zeros to the label of the monetary paper does not alter the fact that the price level in terms of the physical piece of paper is constant. Did France suffer one of the most drastic deflations in history in the late 1950s when one hundred old francs were converted after 1958 into one new franc and prices "fell" to 1 percent of their previous level? It is easy to identify this and other similar monetary conversions with accounting practices of considerable psychological and practical importance, but of no economic interest in a world that abstracts from information costs.

This is not to dismiss Weldon's argument as mere semantics, for he intended his suggestion as a counter example to refute my argument: that even anticipated inflation can have real effects. But the analogue does not apply to an economy in which money bears no interest. It is true that in my model money is being issued at the same rate that prices are rising and that the real value of the depreciation of old money is equal to the real value of newly issued money. But *asset holders do not identify these two events as identical.* In my model the new money *must come into the economy in a manner that dissociates it from existing monetary holdings,* like manna from heaven, dollars from airplanes, or SDRs allocated in proportion to IMF quotas, not existing SDR holdings.

The reason for this is quite obvious, and has many analogies in other parts of economic theory. If tariff proceeds were rebated to individuals pro rata with imports every importer would associate his tariff payment with an equal tariff subsidy, and he would act as if there were no tariff. In the same way Weldon money permits this inadmissible identification with the consequence that the upgrading of money cancels the depreciation of money. If pure inflation is to be analyzed at all, these events must be separated.

Monetary expansion is like stock watering; the stockholders complain and adjust if they know a company is diluting their property rights. The analogy to Weldon money is not, however, stock watering, but a stock split of mere accounting or denominational significance. The idea is well worth recording, however, for it presents the case, of analytical interest, that is the analogue in the context of monetary growth of the homogeneity postulate in a static economy.

CONCLUSION

We have seen that the money rate of interest rises by less than the rate of inflation and therefore the real rate of interest falls during inflation.[10] The conclusion is based on the fact that inflation reduces real money balances and that the resulting decline in wealth stimulates increased saving.[11] Real conditions in the economy are altered by the purely

10. Charles Kennedy, in his "Inflation and the Bond Rate," *Oxford Economic Papers* 12 (Oct. 1960): 269–73, interprets the "Keynesian" solution as an unchanged bond price, an interpretation that does not seem to me to take account of the word "directly" in the passage I have quoted in the introduction. I have tried to show that the change in money interest can be interpreted as being due to a shift in the marginal efficiency schedule as a function of *money* interest, or as a shift in liquidity preference as a function of *real* interest, the former being the solution Keynes presumably had in mind.

11. Although the analysis has concentrated on the division of wealth between money and equities, it can also be expected to apply to an economy in which wealth is held in other forms. Arbitrage will bring relative earnings of bonds in line with the money rate of interest (under the conditions of certainty implied in the theoretical analysis) and "cost-of-living" bonds, an instrument used in many countries accustomed to inflation, will yield a nominal return equal to the real rate of interest plus the rate of inflation. Similarly, foreign exchange will yield a return equal to the rate of inflation, as the domestic exchange rate depreciates, though the initial stock adjustment is complicated by the highly liquid attributes of foreign exchange, which imply that the flight from domestic money will be partly into foreign exchange.

I have analyzed some aspects of this effect in *International Economics* (New York: Macmillan Co., 1968), chap. 19.

monetary phenomenon. The evils or benefits of inflation cannot be attributed solely to the failure of the community to anticipate it.[12]

Foreseeable fluctuations in the rate of inflation can thus have very real effects on economic activity. When prices are expected to rise, the money rate of interest rises by less than the rate of inflation giving impetus to an investment boom and an acceleration of growth. Conversely, when a rise in prices is expected to end, there occurs a stock market slump, a rise in the real rate of interest, and a deceleration of growth.

12. Cf. A. P. Lerner, "The Inflationary Process—Some Theoretical Aspects," *Review of Economics and Statistics* 31 (Aug. 1949): 193–200; reprinted in *Essays in Economic Analysis* (London, 1953): "What is harmful about inflation is not the rise in prices but the failure to anticipate and offset them" (*Essays*, p. 330). This statement would be correct if new money were issued as a proportionate subsidy to existing money balances, because that would amount to the payment of interest on money, reestablishing the proposition of neutrality. In the real world, however, money is not issued in this form.

chapter 3
growth, equilibrium, and the money rate of interest

Our next explicit consideration is growth. This chapter considers the effect of growth on the rate of deflation and the equilibrium of the economy under different assumptions about the rate of monetary expansion; it also points out an error in the interpretation of macroeconomic models and shows how the error can be corrected. The error lies in the assumption that, even when net investment is positive, a constant money stock is compatible with an "equilibrium" interest rate. The equilibrium position itself will be affected by the deflation or changing interest rates necessary to bring about monetary equilibrium. This is because changes in flows affect rates of change of prices which alter expectations, anticipated rates of return, and thus actual asset holdings.

The technical contribution of this chapter is to show how rates of growth and monetary expansion can be explicitly incorporated into the Keynesian or Patinkinian models, preparing the groundwork for a better integration of short-run and long-run analysis.

Adapted from "A Fallacy in the Interpretation of Macroeconomic Equilibrium," *Journal of Political Economy* 73 (Feb. 1965): 61–66, by permission of The University of Chicago Press. Copyright 1965 by the University of Chicago.

DIMENSIONS AND MAGNITUDES

The problem of determining the conditions of monetary equilibrium admits of a comparatively simple solution so long as those terms heretofore considered of the second order of magnitude are neglected. If stock and flow demands for goods, money, and securities balance stock and flow supplies, the interest rate and money income are in equilibrium. It is generally admitted that the equilibrium is not a complete one, since positive savings and investment implies a growing stock of wealth and capital goods and a positive rate of growth of output. But the growth effects are usually dismissed as magnitudes of the second order in the time interval relevant to the short-run equilibrium under consideration.

There does not appear in the literature, however, an explicit justification for the demarcation between magnitudes of the first order and magnitudes of the second order, a distinction that should be an implication, not an assumption, of theory. The implicit rationale for the neglect of rates of change in the context of macroeconomic theory appears to derive from a dimensionality argument. Investment, for example, is dimensionally different from the capital stock; it involves, whereas the capital stock does not, a time dimension. Now if the time interval is made sufficiently short, increments in the stock become negligible in relation to the stock itself. The capital stock grows over time according to the equation

$$K = K_0 e^{(I/K)t},$$

where $I \equiv dK/dt$. Clearly, as $t \to 0$, $K \to K_0$, the initial capital stock. Hence, for short-run analysis, the flow of investment can be disregarded in relation to the capital stock and, by a similar argument, the flows of securities and money can be ignored in relation to the stocks of these assets; the flows are of a second order in relation to the stocks themselves.

Despite the logic of the above argument, flows of capital goods, securities, and money must be explicitly introduced into macroeconomic analysis in order to determine the short-run equilibrium of the interest rate and money income. It is a fallacy to suppose that because flows are infinitesimal in relation to stocks they are of a second order of magnitude with respect to variables incommensurate with the stocks, such as the rate of interest. The rates of change of the capital stock, financial assets, and the money supply are dimensionally equivalent to the rate of interest and cannot be disregarded. Neglect of them in the literature has led to a one-sided and erroneous approach to monetary policy and has concealed theoretical results of great interest.

MONETARY EQUILIBRIUM AND GROWTH

Consider an economy with three types of assets—goods, securities (bonds and equities), and money—held by a consolidated private sector (firms and households) and a consolidated public sector (banks and government). Stock equilibrium requires that the public be willing to hold the existing capital stock; that banks and households be willing to hold the net stock of securities issued by firms and government; and that firms, households, and the government be willing to hold the stock of money issued by the banks. Flow equilibrium requires that any excess of saving over investment of the private sector be matched by an equivalent budget deficit (including net interest payments) of the public sector; that banks and households accumulate the new securities offered by firms and government; and that the public and government hoard the new money created by the banks.

Stock equilibrium is assured by equality of the demand and supply of money explicit in the theory of liquidity preference, and by equality of demand and supply of capital goods implicit in the theory of investment, whereby the stock demand-supply price of capital goods, equal to the marginal discounted product, is brought into equilibrium at any given rate of interest with the flow-supply price of capital goods. Flow equilibrium is insured by the equality of investment and savings (after adjustment for the public sector) and by the equality of new-money creation and hoarding that is a direct implication of equality between the stocks of money demanded and supplied. Together, these conditions imply equality between stocks and flows of securities demanded and supplied.

The important issue is the nature of the equilibrium that is implied by these conditions and whether or not the economic sense of the specific functional relationships making up the system is violated. The demand for money is assumed to depend on the interest rate and money income. Positive investment implies a growing capital stock and, presumably, rising output. If the stock of money is constant and output is rising, monetary equilibrium requires that the price level be falling or that the interest rate be rising. The point at issue is therefore whether falling prices or rising interest rates affect the demand for money or whether they are merely terms of the second order of magnitude.

Suppose that the demand for money varies in direct proportion to money income and in inverse proportion to the interest rate.[1] Monetary

1. This slightly restrictive assumption simplifies the exposition without fundamentally altering the conclusions; the analysis can be made general by allowing for interest and income elasticities of demand for money differing from unity.

equilibrium, together with growth and a constant stock of money, then implies that interest rates are rising or prices are falling at a rate equal to the rate of growth of output. But rates of growth are pure numbers per day, month, or year and have dimensions equivalent to the interest rate. An asset holder would therefore have to weight the importance of a rate of decrease in bond prices equally with the interest rate itself in making portfolio decisions involving choices between money and securities; he would similarly have to take into account the rate of inflation in making portfolio decisions involving the choice between commodities or equities on the one hand, and bonds and money on the other, as shown in the preceding chapter.

It follows that rates of change in commodity and security prices have a first-order impact on the general equilibrium of the system. If monetary equilibrium is established by falling commodity prices, the money interest rate (the nominal yield on bonds and bills) will differ from the real interest rate (the return on equities and the marginal efficiency of capital); whereas, if it is established by falling bond prices, the cost of holding money will differ from the nominal return on bonds by the rate at which bond prices are falling. In both cases the discrepancy between the cost of holding money and the real interest rate causes a shift in the demand for money.

A GEOMETRIC SOLUTION

We can illustrate one solution to the problem of determining equilibrium income by making use of a famous geometric interpretation of macroeconomic equilibrium. The lines *LM* and *IS* (Figure 3-1) are the familiar Hicksian schedules portraying the loci of interest rates and money incomes at which, respectively, money demand equals money supply, and real investment equals real saving. I shall use the configuration to refer to both full employment and unemployment situations; in the full employment case real saving can be assumed to rise with money income because of the (negative) wealth effect of an increased price level on real-money balances; whereas in the unemployment case the Keynesian saving function can be assumed. My results do not depend upon any particular theory underlying the schedules,[2] so I have drawn them with the conventional slopes.

2. For a given employment of the capital stock the ratio of labor to capital rises with the level of output, raising the marginal productivity of capital and hence the rate of growth, for any fraction of income saved, a factor that should be taken into account in constructing the investment schedule. David Meiselman, in a paper presented at the Zurich meeting of the Econometric Society in 1964, explored this theme and discussed its implications for the slope of *IS*; related arguments were made back in 1956 by J. A. Stockfisch and A. J. Steigmann.

There are numerous theoretical difficulties associated with the use of the *IS–LM*

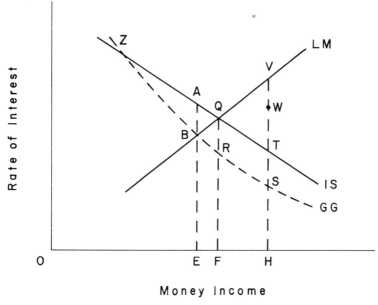

Money Income

Figure 3-1

Growth can be introduced explicitly on the diagram because the growth rate and the interest rate have identical dimensions. A growth schedule *GG* can be constructed such that the vertical distance between *GG* and *IS* measures the rate of growth of output corresponding to each level of saving and investment on *IS*. At some sufficiently high interest rate and low income level saving and investment, and therefore the growth rate, are zero, and *GG* intersects *IS* (at *Z*). At lower interest rates and higher incomes the growth rate is positive. Thus, at the point *A* the rate of growth is assumed to be *AB*, at *Q* it is *QR*, and at *T* it is *TS*.

Consider now the point at the intersection of *IS* and *LM*. *Q* is usually taken to be the equilibrium point. At *Q*, however, the rate of growth of output is *QR*, so that the demand for money can equal the supply of money only if the price level is falling or the interest rate is rising. In both cases the interest rate appropriate for saving-investment decisions will no longer reflect the cost of holding money.

---

configurations involving the possible interdependence of the schedules, the implicit role of the relative price of consumption and investment goods, and the role of expectations in deriving the investment schedule. Since, however, this chapter is restricted to a consideration of the correct equilibrium position itself, it seems legitimate to ignore these difficulties, and adopt the ceteris paribus technique of "holding other fallacies constant." They can be taken into account either by making appropriate shifts in the investment schedule when changes in employment are involved, or by making the level of income itself an argument in the prospective yield on capital in deriving the investment schedule.

There are three essentially equivalent techniques by means of which the equilibrium can be found; they are analogous to the three techniques used for partial equilibrium analysis of an excise tax. The first is to regard the ordinate as the marginal efficiency of capital (on the basis of which investment decisions are made) so that the *IS* schedule remains in position while the *LM* schedule shifts upward by any discrepancy between the real rate of interest and the cost of holding money. The second method is to regard the ordinate as the cost of holding money so that the *LM* schedule is fixed while the *IS* schedule shifts downward by any discrepancy between the money rate of interest and the marginal efficiency of capital. In the first case the intersection of the *IS* schedule and the shifted *LM* schedule determines the marginal efficiency of capital, and in the second case the intersection of the *LM* schedule and the shifted *IS* schedule determines the cost of holding money.

The third method, and the one I shall use, is to regard the ordinate, for purposes of deriving the *LM* schedule, as the cost of holding money, so that *LM* remains fixed; and to regard the ordinate, for purposes of deriving the *IS* schedule, as the marginal efficiency of capital, so that *IS* too remains fixed. The equilibrium is then discovered by finding the level of money income at which the vertical distance between the *IS* and *LM* schedules equals the difference between the cost of holding money and the marginal efficiency of capital.

The true equilibrium is most easily interpreted if we analyze the extreme cases where commodity prices fall and where bond prices fall separately. If at Q commodity prices were falling at a rate sufficient for the real quantity of money to increase at the same rate as output, that is, at the rate QR, the cost of holding money would be FR, not FQ, since the rate of decline in the prices of commodities and equities (QR) would reduce the cost of holding money with respect to commodities and equities by an equal amount. At Q asset-holders would sell equities and try to acquire more money and bonds, and this would raise the real rate of interest and lower the money rate of interest to the point where real yields on all assets are equalized. Equilibrium, therefore, requires a discrepancy between the real and money rates of interest equal to the rate of deflation, which in turn must equal the rate of growth. This is possible only at the point where GG intersects LM at B. At this equilibrium the level of income is OE, the money rate of interest is EB, the real rate of interest is EA, and both the rate of growth and the rate of deflation are AB.

A similar analysis holds if interest rates, instead of commodity prices, adapt to preserve equality between money demand and supply. Q cannot be the equilibrium point because at Q bond prices would be falling, reducing the opportunity cost of holding money. If bond prices fall at the same rate that output is growing, the cost of holding money is again *FR*, not *FQ*, and true equilibrium is again at the income level *OE*.

The interpretation of the new equilibrium in the case of falling bond prices (rising interest rates) is somewhat different from the preceding example of falling commodity prices. There is no gap between the real and money rates of interest since all rates of interest are expressed, when the price level is constant, in real terms. *EA* represents the bond rate of interest and the return on equities while *EB* represents the bond rate of interest less the rate at which the interest rate is rising. The gap between the bond rate and the cost of holding money arises from the capital losses associated with holding bonds.

The interest rate *EB* can be interpreted as the short-term rate of interest. It is the yield on bills of virtually zero duration because the price of bills must reflect both the nominal bond interest rate and the depreciating capital value of bonds. At the equilibrium income *OE*, therefore, the short-term interest rate is lower and the long-term interest rate is higher than at *Q*. Instead of a gap between money and real rates of interest there is a gap between short-term and long-term rates of interest.[3]

THE RATE OF MONETARY EXPANSION

It has now been established that, if the rate of monetary expansion is zero, the price of goods or bonds must fall under the assumed conditions, at a rate equal to the rate of growth of output, *AB*, and that the equilibrium income is *OE*, not *OF*. Similar reasoning shows that there is a different position of equilibrium for each given rate of monetary expansion. When the latter is negative, equilibrium income is less than *OE*, and when it is positive income is greater than *OE*.

The position of equilibrium is in all cases at the level of income where the rate of monetary expansion is equal to the vertical distance between *LM* and *GG*. With a rate of monetary expansion equal to *QR*

3.   The link between a changing interest rate or price level and the demand for assets (including real-money balances) is of course expectational: asset-holders are assumed to expect current rates of change to continue. The *duration* of the expectation is, however, crucial in determining the prevailing crescendo of interest rates since, obviously, a given rate of change of commodity, equity, or bond prices that is expected to persist for only, say, a few months would produce a structure of rates higher at the short end of the maturity scale relative to the structure produced by rates of change expected to persist for several years. In order to draw sharper lines in this discussion, I have assumed implicitly in the text that rates of change are expected to persist indefinitely, in which case the "short-term rate" reflects the instantaneous rate of interest and the "long-term rate" reflects the rate on consols. I have not taken explicit account of the effect of capital gains arising from changing bond prices on the rate of saving.

(the rate of growth at the income level *OF*) equilibrium is at *Q* and the price level and the interest rate are constant. The point *Q*, the conventional interpretation of equilibrium, can therefore be regarded as the true equilibrium if the rate of monetary expansion equals the rate of growth of output. In other words, the traditional exposition of macroeconomic equilibrium can be used provided it is specified that the money supply is growing rapidly enough to satisfy the growing demand for money.

Consider now a situation in which the rate of monetary expansion exceeds the rate of growth of output. If the rate of monetary expansion is *SV* (greater than the rate of growth *TS*), the equilibrium income is *OH*. Then, regardless of whether commodity prices are fixed or flexible, *HV* will reflect the short-term rate of interest (the cost of holding money) and *VT* the excess of the rate of monetary expansion over the rate of growth. But if prices are flexible, *HV* can also be identified with both the long-term rate of interest and the money rate of interest, and *VT* with both the rate of inflation and the excess of the money rate of interest over the real rate of interest.[4] If, however, the price level is fixed, *HT* will be the long-term rate of interest, and *VT* both the rate at which the long-term rate of interest is falling and the excess of the short-term interest rate over the existing long-term rate. In both cases the rate of monetary expansion *SV* establishes the equilibrium income *OH*.[5]

Equilibrium would probably, in the real world, be preserved by movements in both bond prices and commodity and equity prices, the division between which is intimately bound up with anticipations, the state of employment, and the conjuncture of the business cycle. For example, the rate of monetary expansion *VS* at the equilibrium income *OH* might be divided between the rate of growth equal to *ST*, a rate of inflation equal to *WT*, and a rate of increase in bond prices equal to *WV*; in that case the nominal return on equities would be *HT*, on bonds *HW*, and on bills *HV*, despite the fact that bonds, bills, and equities all yield the same commodity rate of return of *HT*.

The essential conclusion to be drawn, however, concerns not the determination of the precise pattern of real and money rates of interest on short- and long-term securities to which the rate of monetary expansion

4. In chapter 2, above, I analyzed this case, noting (correctly) that "the inflation itself is generated by monetary expansion *in excess of growth*."

5. Notice that this analysis has been concerned solely with various *states* of growth equilibrium and not with the dynamic problem of actually moving from one state of growth equilibrium to another, a problem which is complicated by the entangling of two basically different types of expectation, namely, those engendered by the extrapolation of various rates of expansion at a state of growth equilibrium and those generated by the actual (finite) changes in the level of equilibrium income in the transition from one growth equilibrium to another.

Note also that in an open economy the money supply would become an endogenous variable given by the balance of payments. On this see my *International Economics* (New York: Macmillan Co., 1968), chap. 9.

gives rise, but rather the central role of the rate of monetary expansion itself, operating through its influence on anticipations and asset prices, in determining the equilibrium level of money income. This role is entirely distinct from concepts of the role of monetary policy which attach sole importance to alterations in the stock of monetary assets.

chapter 4

deficit finance and growth

We now turn to a consideration of fiscal policy combined with monetary policy. This chapter considers the effect of monetary expansion on equilibrium when the monetary expansion is used to finance government deficits, used in turn to finance economic growth. Its theoretical contribution lies in its synthesis of growth analysis with the quantity theory of money.

The argument for inflationary finance as an efficient vehicle of economic development has never been convincingly validated in theory, but it has, nevertheless, occupied an important position in the thinking of policy planners in some less developed countries. This raises the theoretical question of the extent to which the inflation-growth argument is valid and relevant.

It is generally accepted that governments can squeeze *some* resources out of the private sector by deficit finance and thereby generate extra government capital formation. This is because inflation, defined in the sense of monetary expansion, is a tax—as classical economists like John Mill were well aware. Just as a counterfeiter can take away resources from his compatriots, so can the government. To the extent that the resources taken by the government from the community are obtained at the expense of private

Adapted from "Growth, Stability and Inflationary Finance," *Journal of Political Economy* 73 (Apr. 1965): 97–109, by permission of The University of Chicago Press. Copyright 1965 by the University of Chicago.

consumption and invested in productive capital, growth can be accelerated. Or even if the tax is at the expense of private investment, growth could be accelerated if the marginal social rate of return on government investment exceeded the return on private investment.

An evaluation of the arguments for inflation as a vehicle for development finance, however, cannot be completed until the total effects of the inflation on the society are taken into account. The fact that social capital can be augmented by inflationary finance is not a convincing argument unless it is also shown that the inflation tax is more efficient than alternative taxes, or that its "burden" is less inequitable. As Bailey showed, inflation has a pure welfare cost which has to be compared to the welfare cost of other taxes. Moreover, inflation has unmeasurable costs and benefits associated with the capital markets, the substitution of other forms of money, payments habits, and the political system itself. For these reasons, caution has to be exercised in accepting arguments based on economic criteria alone.

This chapter concludes on a note of pessimism about the economic virtues of an inflation tax, particularly since no account has been taken of the resource misallocation that often accompanies inflation. On the other hand, no attempt has been made to allow for possibly favorable employment effects which, even if temporary, may for a time provide a spur to development, or for political costs and benefits which the economist as social scientist cannot explicitly measure. The orientation of this chapter is not toward these practical social questions, but to the resource issues alone.

THE GROWTH EFFECTS OF INFLATIONARY FINANCE

From the equation of exchange

$$MV = PY, \tag{1}$$

where M = the money supply; V = velocity; P = price level; and Y = output, we have, by differentiation with respect to time, the identity

$$\frac{1}{V}\frac{dV}{dt} = \pi + \lambda - \rho, \tag{2}$$

where $\pi = (1/P)(dP/dt)$ = rate of inflation; $\lambda = (1/Y)(dY/dt)$ = rate of growth; and $\rho = (1/M)(dM/dt)$ = rate of monetary expansion. From the relation between output and capital

$$Y = \phi K, \tag{3}$$

where ϕ = productivity of capital and K = capital stock, we have also

$$\frac{dY}{dt} = \phi \frac{dK}{dt},\tag{4}$$

where ϕ is assumed to be constant.

Suppose that the central bank finances all government investment and that all other investment is ignored. Then the real value of government investment is[1]

$$\frac{G}{P} = \frac{1}{P}\frac{dR}{dt} = \frac{dK}{dt},\tag{5}$$

where R = bank reserves and G = government investment. The relation between bank reserves and the money supply is

$$R = rM,\tag{6}$$

where r = the fractional reserve ratio if pocket currency is ignored. The result of differentiating equation (6), that is,

$$\frac{dR}{dt} = r\frac{dM}{dt},\tag{7}$$

can then be substituted into equation (5) to give

$$\frac{dK}{dt} = r\frac{1}{P}\frac{dM}{dt}\tag{8}$$

and equation (8) in turn can be put into equation (4) to yield

$$\frac{dY}{dt} = r\phi\frac{1}{P}\frac{dM}{dt}.\tag{9}$$

Dividing equation (9) by Y gives

$$\frac{1}{Y}\frac{dY}{dt} = r\phi\frac{1}{PY}\frac{dM}{dt} = r\phi\left(\frac{1}{M}\frac{dM}{dt}\right)\frac{M}{PY},\tag{10}$$

which expresses a relation between the rate of growth and the rate of monetary expansion:

$$\lambda = \frac{r\phi}{V}\rho,\tag{11}$$

---

1. The last part of this equation assumes that private investment is zero and is unaffected by the inflation. But credit-financed public investment would probably be partly at the expense of private investment. To the extent that this is so, the assumption unduly favors the inflationist argument and therefore strengthens my own conclusions.

remembering that λ = rate of growth; ϕ = productivity of capital; r = fractional reserve ratio; V = income velocity; and ρ = rate of monetary expansion.

During a time interval in which velocity is constant, we have, instead of (2), the equation

$$\pi = \rho - \lambda, \tag{12}$$

into which (11) can be substituted to give either

$$\pi = \left(1 - \frac{r\phi}{V}\right)\rho \tag{13}$$

or

$$\pi = \left(\frac{V}{r\phi} - 1\right)\lambda. \tag{14}$$

These equations relate the rate of inflation to the rate of monetary expansion and the rate of growth induced by deficit finance.[2]

The meaning of these results can be clarified by regarding $1/V$ as the *desired* ratio of money to income and considering an interval of time during which the government spends r units of bank reserves on capital goods. At constant prices this implies capital formation of r units and therefore an increase in output of $r\phi$ units. But an increase in output of *one* unit would increase the demand for money by $1/V$ units, so that an increase in output of $r\phi$ units increases the demand for money by $r\phi/V$ units. Meanwhile, the increase in bank reserves of r units increases the supply of money by 1 unit. Hence, at constant prices, the demand for money goes up by $r\phi/V$ units, while the supply of money goes up by 1 unit. This means that there is an excess demand or supply of money according to whether $r\phi/V$ is greater or less than unity. Deficit financing is thus inflationary or deflationary according to whether

$$V \gtrless r\phi, \tag{15}$$

that is, according to whether velocity is greater than or less than the product of the fractional reserve ratio and the productivity of capital.

As a practical matter, deficit financing is always inflationary. The income velocity of money is a multiple of unity, and both ϕ and r are fractions of unity. In fact, the ratio $r\phi/V$ is nothing more than the ratio of bank reserves to the capital stock, a dimensionless fraction which is

---

2.   It should be observed that V and ϕ have the same dimensions, while r is dimensionless so that the ratios in equations (13) and (14) are dimensionless.

always—in every conceivable country—less than unity. But before introducing empirical considerations it is necessary to elaborate on the behavior of velocity during inflation.

INFLATION AND VELOCITY

The simplest hypothesis, that velocity is constant, is clearly inadmissible when different rates of inflation are involved. The rate of inflation is itself part of the cost of holding real-money balances. The higher the rate of inflation, the smaller the quantity of real-money balances the community would want to hold. This amounts to saying that velocity is an increasing function[3] of the inflation rate:

$$V = V(\pi), \tag{16}$$

where $V'(\pi) > 0$.

Assuming tentatively that the relation between velocity and inflation is linear, (16) can be written as follows:

$$V = V_0 + \eta\pi, \tag{17}$$

where V_0 is the rate of velocity at a zero rate of inflation. If this equation is then combined with

$$\pi = \left(\frac{V}{r\phi} - 1\right)\lambda, \tag{14}$$

we have two equations in the variables π and V in addition to the policy-determined[4] parameter λ. These equations are plotted in Figure 4-1, for the growth rate λ_1.

---

3. More precisely, velocity is a function of the money rate of interest. In chapter 2, above, I took account of effects of wealth which can increase saving and lower the real rate of interest under anticipated inflation, with the result that the money rate of interest rises by less than the rate of inflation. This effect is ignored in the present chapter (which implicitly assumes that the real rate of interest is constant) so that the money rate of interest rises by the rate of inflation. This simplification could perhaps be justified in an economy in which capital goods and consumer goods can be produced (or bought from abroad) at constant real opportunity costs, although it neglects the possibility that the productivity of capital may itself be an increasing function of the ratio of real money to capital (attributing to money a physical marginal productivity as a factor of production). In the latter case my conclusions would again be strengthened (see chapter 5).

4. Strictly speaking, the authorities have control over only one side of the transaction, the offer of reserve money, while the public has "control" over the other side, the goods or factor services obtained in exchange for it. Hence λ is a "policy determined parameter" only up to the limit discussed below. On the other hand, ρ is entirely determined by policy, and equilibrium in Figure 4-1 could be determined by plotting equation (14) instead of equation (13); in that case a $\rho_1\rho_1$ line would replace $\lambda_1\lambda_1$, and its slope would progressively increase as the rate of inflation rises, becoming asymptotic to a vertical line representing the given rate of monetary expansion.

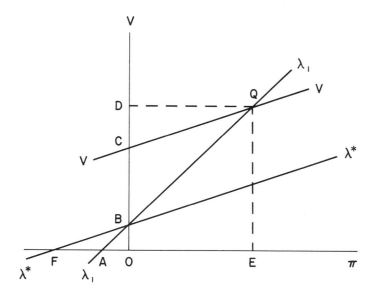

Figure 4-1   To achieve the growth rate $\lambda_1 = OA$, a rate of reserve (and monetary) expansion of AE is required, resulting in a rate of inflation of OE and an increase in velocity of CD. Equilibrium for higher growth rates than λ_1 is found by pivoting $\lambda\lambda$ lines clockwise about point B, where OB is the product of the banking reserve ratio and the productivity of capital. After $\lambda\lambda$ acquires the same slope as VV, further growth cannot be achieved by deficit finance. Maximum growth rate is OF.

To solve equations (17) and (14) for π by means of the diagram, note that the level of π at the equilibrium Q is

$$\pi = OE = DQ = \frac{BC}{BC/DQ} = \frac{OC - OB}{BC/DQ}$$

$$= \frac{OC - OB}{(BD - CD)/DQ} = \frac{OC - OB}{(BD/DQ) - (CD/DQ)}$$

$$= \frac{OC - OB}{(OB/OA) - (CD/DQ)} = \left[\frac{OC - OB}{(OB - [CD/DQ])OA} \right] OA.$$

The following relations are evident from the construction of the graph:[5]

$$V_0 = OC; \quad r\phi = OB; \quad \lambda_1 = OA; \quad \eta = \frac{CD}{DQ}.$$

5.   Equation (14) can alternatively be written as $V = r\phi (1 + \pi/\lambda)$ or $\lambda = r\phi\pi/V - r\phi$, so that when $\pi = 0$, $V = r\phi$; and when $V = 0$, $\lambda = -\pi$.

It then follows from substitution that

$$\pi = \frac{V_0 - r\phi}{r\phi - \eta\lambda}\, \lambda = \left[\frac{(V_0/r\phi) - 1}{1 - (\eta/r\phi)\lambda}\right]\lambda, \tag{18}$$

a result that could be obtained by substituting equation (17) into equation (14).

It is apparent from equation (18) that π is not a linear function of λ. The ratio π/λ increases with λ. This means that the greater the growth rate financed by reserve creation, the larger will be marginal increments of the inflation rate. A limit will eventually be reached at which the inflation rate approaches infinity, which is another way of saying that further growth cannot be achieved by deficit finance. In the diagram this limit is reached when the $\lambda\lambda$ line, which pivots about the point B for the different growth rates (getting flatter as the growth rate becomes higher), is parallel to VV, in the position $\lambda^*\lambda^*$. The corresponding growth rate (which is purely hypothetical because $\pi = \infty$ is inadmissible) is

$$\lambda^* = OF = \frac{OB}{OB/OF} = \frac{OB}{DC/DQ},$$

since, when VV is parallel to $\lambda^*\lambda^*$, $OB/OF = DC/DQ$. It follows that the maximum growth rate is

$$\lambda^* = \frac{r\phi}{\eta}. \tag{19}$$

This is the value of λ when the denominator of equation (18) is zero. It can be regarded as the upper limit on credit-financed growth.

EMPIRICAL IMPORTANCE OF
MONEY-FINANCED GROWTH

Income velocities at low or zero rates of inflation are typically between 3 and 5, capital-output ratios range between 2 and 5, and fractional-reserve ratios of banks usually vary between $\frac{1}{10}$ and $\frac{3}{10}$.[6] From equation (18)—repeated for convenience—

$$\pi = \frac{V_0 - r\phi}{r\phi - \eta\lambda}\, \lambda, \tag{18}$$

6. For income velocities see J. J. Polak and L. Boissonneault, "Monetary Analysis of Income and Imports," *IMF Staff Papers*, Nov. 1957; for a sample of capital-output ratios see *Income and Wealth* vol. 8 (National Bureau of Economic Research); and for banking reserve ratios see J. Ahrensdorf and S. Kanesathasan, "Variations in the Money Multiplier and Their Implications for Central Banking," *IMF Staff Papers*, Nov. 1960.

it is clear that low values of V_0 and η, and high values of r and ϕ, are favorable to the inflation thesis in the sense that relatively low inflation rates will be associated with given growth rates. If we then choose values which are the most favorable conceivable for the inflation-growth argument (i.e., if we choose lower limits of V_0 and upper limits of ϕ and r), and set $V_0 = 3$, $\phi = \frac{1}{2}$, and $r = \frac{3}{10}$, equation (18) becomes

$$\pi = \frac{57}{3 - 20\eta\lambda}\lambda. \tag{20}$$

In the special case where $\eta = 0$ (which is equivalent to the assumption that velocity is unaffected by the rate of inflation) the result is

$$\pi = 19\lambda, \tag{21}$$

which states that the inflation rate is nineteen times the credit-financed growth rate. To increase the growth rate by one percentage point per year, for example, would result in an inflation of 19 percent per year, on the assumption that velocity is unaffected.

Velocity will, of course, be increased by inflation in any actual situation. It appears reasonable to assume that velocity will eventually double well before an expected 30 percent inflation is reached.[7] On this assumption, in addition to the assumption that $V_0 = 3$, a *lower* limit of $\eta = 10$ can be calculated.

Substituting this value into equation (20) gives

$$\pi = \frac{57\lambda}{3 - 200\lambda}. \tag{22}$$

From equation (22) it is clear that the upper limit on growth is $\frac{3}{200} = .015$, or 1.5 percent, and this is associated with an "infinite inflation." Intermediate values are given in the table below.

From these calculations it should be evident that the growth argument for inflationary finance is not, apparently, a strong one. Even in the case where the values of the parameters are purposely chosen to make the inflation argument appear favorable, inflation rates of over 50 percent per year are necessary to add 1 percent to the growth rate.

7. For example, velocity doubled between 1940 and 1958 in Chile as the bank rate of interest doubled and the rate of inflation moved from an average of 15 percent in 1940–45 to an increase of about 45 percent in the period 1953–58. Again, in the case of Taiwan, velocity fell from 11.7 in 1951, when inflation was 30 percent, to 9 percent in 1956, when inflation was 17 percent; and then velocity moved down to 7.7 when inflation fell again to 7 percent.

AN ALTERNATIVE ASSUMPTION

It is worth trying a form of the velocity function other than the linear one, $V = V_0 + \eta\pi$. Philip Cagan has found successful fits of an equation of a form similar to

$$V = V_0 e^{a\pi} \tag{23}$$

for hyperinflations.[8] If this relation is substituted into (14) we have

$$\pi = \left(\frac{V_0 e^{a\pi}}{r\phi} - 1 \right) \lambda, \tag{24}$$

and if it is put into (11) the result is

$$\lambda = \frac{r\phi}{V_0 e^{a\pi}} \rho. \tag{25}$$

ANNUAL PERCENTAGE RATES

Growth Rate	Inflation Rate
0.25	5.7
0.50	14.25
0.75	28.5
1.00	57.0
1.25	142.5
1.50	∞

In this case it is clear that growth reaches a maximum at a finite rate of inflation. Differentiation of equation (25) with respect to ρ and

8. Philip Cagan, "The Monetary Dynamics of Hyperinflation," in *Studies in the Quantity Theory of Money*, ed. M. Friedman (Chicago, 1956), pp. 25–121. Cagan's function is $M/P = e^{-aE-\gamma}$, where E is the expected rate of inflation and a and γ are constants, which is easily converted into (23) if the output "elasticity" of demand for money is assumed to be unity.

Equation (23) implies that the velocity has no upper limit. The traditional assumption of an upper limit depends on rigidities in payments periods, but Cagan's work shows that these payments periods become shorter during hyperinflation. Thus velocity may have an upper limit *given* the payments period, but none when the latter adapts to the inflation. It should be mentioned, however, that Cagan's results (as he explains) were unsatisfactory in the higher reaches of hyperinflation, so velocity may have an upper limit after all, though a much higher one than previously imagined.

setting $d\lambda/d\pi = 0$ gives the rate of monetary expansion at which growth is maximized:[9]

$$\rho^* = \frac{1}{a},\tag{26}$$

after making the substitution $d\rho/d\pi = 1$, which follows from $\pi + \lambda = \rho$ when $d\lambda/d\rho = 0$. Substituting equation (26) into equation (25) and using the resulting expression to eliminate λ from equation (24) gives the growth-maximizing rate of inflation

$$\pi^* = \frac{1}{a}\left(1 - \frac{r\phi}{V_0 e^{a\pi}}\right).\tag{27}$$

To illustrate the implications of the inflation argument when Cagan's velocity function is used, consider the following values for the parameters: $r = 1$; $a = 3$; $\phi = \frac{1}{4}$; $V_0 = 4$. The velocity function in that case is $V = 4e^{3\pi}$. This is illustrated by the following schedule:

Inflation Rate (π) (Percent)	Velocity (V)
0	4.0
10	5.4
20	7.3
30	9.8
40	13.3
50	17.9

Substituting the parameters into equation (27) gives

$$\pi^* = \frac{1}{3}\left[1 - \left(\frac{1}{48\,e^{3\pi}}\right)\right],\tag{28}$$

which has an approximate solution $\pi = .325$, or 32.5 percent. The growth-maximizing inflation rate is therefore 32.5 percent. But the important point is that this inflation rate results in an increment in growth of only $\lambda = \rho - \pi = .333 - .325 = .008$ or $\frac{4}{5}$ of 1 percent (recalling that $\rho = 1/a = \frac{1}{3}$

9. Cagan (op. cit., pp. 77–86) computes the maximum revenue from the "tax on cash balances" implied by the inflation as occurring at the point where $\pi = 1/a$ because he assumes no growth. Martin Bailey, in "The Welfare Cost of Inflationary Finance," *Journal of Political Economy* 66 (Apr. 1956), argues that inflation has a welfare cost, and, using Cagan's data, computes the points at which the marginal welfare cost balances the marginal revenue from the tax.

when growth is at a maximum). And this example derives from a favorable assumption that the banking reserve ratio is 1.[10]

10. In principle, of course, the authorities could require 100 percent reserve ratios. Martin Bailey has suggested, as an alternative, that the authorities could permit or require the banks to pay interest on demand deposits equal to the rate of inflation.

I am grateful to L. Harris for finding the approximate solution of equation (28).

chapter 5

inflation, hoarding, and the stationary state

This chapter integrates short-run, inter-run, and long-run effects of inflation studied in preceding chapters by taking into account the portfolio, hoarding, and accumulation effects of inflation on saving, growth, and the productivity of capital. It shows that a given rate of monetary expansion will have a less inflationary effect in the inter-run because it causes real hoarding associated with the increase in the savings ratio and growth rate. The cash intensity of the economy and thus the real rate of interest will fall by less than if the growth effect on real hoarding were not considered.

In the advance to the stationary state the marginal product of capital falls as accumulation proceeds because the diminishing rate of saving reduces the rate of growth and real hoarding, increasing the rate of inflation associated with a given monetary expansion and lowering financial intensity and the marginal product of capital. At the stationary state real wealth will have been restored, but real cash will be lower and the capital stock higher than before the inflation was introduced.

MONETARY EQUILIBRIUM

In the economy to be investigated below, balance requires equilibrium in two markets: a market for claims (against money) and a market for capital (against money). In choosing between stocks of money, claims, and capital, the typical investor balances expected yields on each asset. Expectations are assumed to be based on an extrapolation of current rates of change; thus, if prices of commodities are rising at the rate π it is assumed that they will go on rising at that rate, and similarly for changes in the prices of claims. This assumption enables us to isolate important comparative dynamic properties of the economic system under conditions of inflation and to develop a convenient representation of it in graphical form.

The line ii in Figure 5-1 refers to the money-claims market in which the nominal interest rate is taken to be a declining function of real money balances plotted on the abscissa. At low interest rates the community is willing to hold the outstanding stock of securities only if the quantity of real money balances is high. When the rate of interest rises people shift out of money into claims, raising the price level and lowering the real value of money balances. We shall write this function as

$$i = i(m), \tag{1}$$

where $m = M/P$, the real value of money holdings, and i is the rate of interest paid on claims. The negative slope is simply a reflection of diminishing returns.

The rr schedule plots the relation between the real interest rate and the stock of real money balances at which the money-capital market is in equilibrium. For a given quantity of real capital, an increase in real money balances raises the proportion of liquidity to capital and thus the marginal product of capital. The real rate of interest can thus be considered an

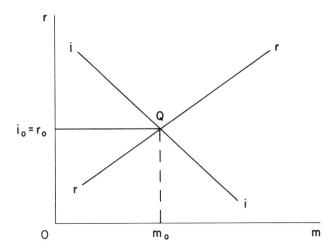

Figure 5-1   The Static Equilibrium

increasing function of the quantity of real balances. We shall write this function in the form

$$r = r(m), \tag{2}$$

where r is the real rate of interest.

The equilibrium interest rate and level of real balances is determined, in the absence of growth of capital or money, by the intersection of the two schedules, ii and rr, at the point Q. The equilibrium condition

$$i(m) = r(m) \tag{3}$$

determines the equilibrium level of real money balances, m_0. At levels of real money balances lower than m_0 the marginal product of real capital is lower than the marginal product of money, and asset holders would shift out of commodities into money, lowering the price level and raising the quantity of real-money balances. To put the adjustment process differently, raising the rate of interest above r_0 would create an excess supply of money and capital and an excess demand for securities, inducing a fall in the rate of interest and a return to the equilibrium at Q. Thus Q is a stable equilibrium.

GROWTH

Now let us consider saving and growth: the acquisition of money and capital assets. Saving is allocated between additional liquidity (hoarding) and capital, and thus implies an increase in spending on goods smaller than the change in real output. If it is measured as a rate of change it can be deducted from the rr line to get a new schedule like $\lambda\lambda$ (see Figure 5-2). For simplicity of exposition we shall also identify this schedule with the rate of growth of output, although this is strictly valid only if the income elasticity of demand for real balances is equal to unity.

When the economy is growing but the stock of money is constant, the equilibrium would be at R. Monetary equilibrium in general requires that the price level be falling at a rate equal to the difference between the rate of capital growth and monetary growth, while capital market equilibrium requires that the real rate of interest be higher than the nominal rate of interest by the deflation rate $-\pi = RT$ when the stock of money is constant. Thus

$$i\left(\frac{M}{P}\right) - r\left(\frac{M}{P}\right) = \pi \tag{4}$$

and

$$\rho = \pi + \lambda \tag{5}$$

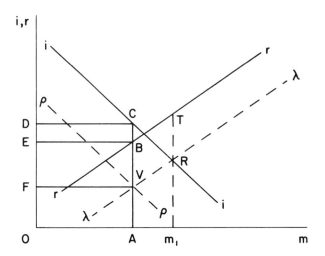

Figure 5-2   Inflationary Growth Equilibrium

with

$$\rho = \rho_0 \tag{6}$$

where π is the rate of inflation, λ is the given rate of growth, and ρ is the rate of monetary expansion. When $\rho = 0$, $\pi = -\lambda$, and the economy will experience deflation. Holders of money and claims to nominal income streams will receive capital gains equal to the rate of deflation.

Now consider the effects of a positive rate of monetary expansion. This can be represented on the diagram by drawing a line $\rho\rho$ beneath the schedule ii such that the vertical distance between the two schedules $\rho\rho$ and ii represents the rate of monetary expansion. The equilibrium level of real money balances will then be determined by the value of the abscissa at the point where $\rho\rho$ and $\lambda\lambda$ intersect. Thus, for the $\rho\rho$ schedule drawn in the diagram, a new equilibrium is reached at V. The equilibrium is characterized by the following phenomena:

$r = OE$ = the real interest rate
$i = OD$ = the money interest rate
$\rho = FD$ = the rate of monetary expansion
$\lambda = FE$ = the rate of growth
$\pi = BC$ = the rate of inflation

The comparative "statics" of the system are readily established. An increase in the rate of monetary expansion lowers the real interest rate, raises the money interest rate, and lowers the level of real-money balances.

This is readily seen formally by differentiating the above system with respect to ρ_0 and noting that $\partial i/\partial(M/P) < 0$ and $\partial r/\partial(M/P) > 0$.

ACCUMULATION AND SYNTHESIS OF EFFECTS

We shall now consider the effects of accumulation. It will be convenient to make a slight alteration in the graphical apparatus: instead of using real money balances on the abscissa we substitute real money balances *per unit of the capital stock* and assume that output is produced under conditions of constant returns to scale according to the production function

$$x = x(m, k) \tag{7}$$

or

$$\frac{x}{k} = x\left(\frac{m}{k}, 1\right) \tag{8}$$

where $m \equiv M/P$ is the real value of money balances.

Figure 5-3 duplicates the essentials of Figure 5-2 with the modification of the interpretation of the abscissa, the money-capital ratio. For the given rate of monetary expansion $\rho\rho$ and the rate of hoarding specified by $\lambda_2\lambda_2$, the inter-run equilibrium of the economy implies a money-capital ratio OA.

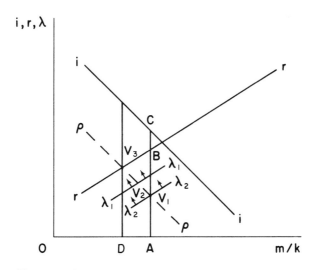

Figure 5-3

Long run accumulation can now be allowed for. As wealth increases saving declines, and the reduction in saving is divided between a reduction in real capital formation and hoarding. This means that the $\lambda_2\lambda_2$ line shifts gradually upward, and the equilibrium of the economy is determined by a moving point sailing up the $\rho\rho$ line through the points V_1 and V_2 until V_3, where $\lambda\lambda$ coincides with rr, is reached. The stationary equilibrium of the economy is at the money-capital ratio OD; in the trip to the stationary state the rate of inflation gradually increases asymptotically to the rate of monetary expansion.

Let us now summarize the results reached by recapitulating short-run, inter-run, and long-run elements in the adjustment process. To simplify let us start from a position of steady-state equilibrium at the point Q in Figure 5-4. Let this equilibrium now be disturbed by a rate of monetary expansion ρ_1 equal to QJ.

The *short run* is that period in which portfolios and expectations adjust to the disturbance; the rate of monetary expansion increases spending power and thus spending. The *spending effect* induces a rise in prices and expectations of inflation. The *expectations effect* causes the public to change its attitude about optimal money holdings, leading to a *velocity* or *portfolio effect* as the public flees from cash into goods, bidding up the price level until portfolios have been adjusted to the desired ratio.

There will be a *secondary expectations effect* arising from the inflation intrinsic to the portfolio effect and leading to a temporary overadjustment of portfolio balances (excessive rise in velocity), but apart from inter-run and long-run effects, adjustment would result in a situation in which the

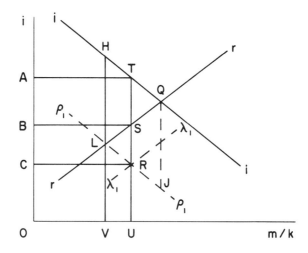

Figure 5-4

community would expect prices to rise at a rate equal to ρ_1. Thus equilibrium in the short run implies a money-capital ratio equal to OV.

The *inter run* is that period in which growth plans are made and implemented. Before that point occurs, however, there is an inter-run effect that has to be taken into account. The flight from money reduces wealth, which stimulates saving, part of which is manifested in real hoarding. This *hoarding effect* slows the price inflation and results in an inter-run growth equilibrium with a money-capital ratio equal to OU, determined by the hoarding rate RT, the vertical distance between ii and $\lambda_1\lambda_1$. Thus the inter-run hoarding effect mitigates the short-run portfolio effect, damping the initial inflation rate.

The *long run* is the period during which adjustment of the capital stock is allowed for. As accumulation proceeds, saving declines, the growth-hoarding effect dies out, and the rate of inflation increases, decreasing the cash intensity.

On our assumption that rates of return depend only on the *ratio* of money and capital, the money-capital ratio in the new stationary position will be the same as that arising from the short-run portfolio effect. But the absolute levels of the capital stock and real-money stock will be different; there is an *accumulation effect*. The capital stock will be *higher* than before the inflation, while the real-money stock will be *lower*. The equilibrium money stock will be larger, however, than just after its initial destruction due to the portfolio effect.

If the monetary expansion is now stopped, the adjustment will move in reverse. Monetary tightness will slow inflation, expectations will be revised, and the demand for real balances will increase. People will adjust their portfolios in order to have more money. Unless the quantity of money is increased, the flight from goods will cause deflation and thus a secondary expectations effect. After these effects have been worked out the community will be wealthier than before.

If wealth were at the desired level before the cessation of the inflation, wealth would now be above the desired level, and dissaving would commence. A retrogression would set in, beginning with a gradual downward adjustment of the capital stock until the original level of wealth were restored. The combination of the portfolio effect in the short run, the hoarding effect arising out of new saving in the inter run, and the dis-accumulation effect in the long run would lead us back to the original equilibrium position. It is easy to see that a period of monetary expansion followed by a period of contraction could induce fluctuations of real investment and the stock of capital reminiscent of the Austrian theory of the cycle in the form put forth by Friedrich Hayek. Superimposed on the long-run cycle would be short-run and inter-run cycles caused by adjustment in expectations and portfolios.

In the real world, of course, many processes are not reversible—or are so only after decades or even centuries; inflations no doubt have an impact on population and knowledge cycles. In the period of time spanned by most policy considerations knowledge accumulation interrupts the reversibility of inflation, and presumably leaves a permanent impact on the capital stock, tastes, and morals.

MONEY IN PRODUCTION AND CONSUMPTION

Let us now conclude this chapter by distinguishing between the roles of money as a consumption good and a production good to see whether this distinction is likely to alter the conclusions of the preceding theory. We can distinguish between money qua consumer asset and money qua factor of production. The institutional counterparts of this distinction are money balances held by households and firms.[1]

To sharpen the distinction between money as a factor and money as a good let us assume that real output is a function of the money balances held by firms while liquidity services, measured in commodity units, to consumers are a function only of money balances held by households. We can represent the system by five equations:

$$l = l(m_h, k_h) \tag{9}$$

where l denotes liquidity services produced in conjunction with household capital, k_h, and household cash, m_h;

$$x = x(m_f, k_f) \tag{10}$$

where x denotes output produced by the cash and capital of firms. For short-run analysis we can assume that the stock of physical capital in the economy as a whole and its distribution between firms and households are fixed. This means that money balances held by firms and households alike will produce liquidity and commodity services under conditions of diminishing returns.

The household demand for liquidity and commodity services is determined by maximizing the utility function of households, while the firms' supply function is given by maximization of the capitalized value of profits.

---

1. Keynes made this distinction in his separation of the motives for holding cash into the income motive, the business motive, the precautionary motive, and the speculative motive, and his classification of the first two motives into income deposits and business deposits; the latter two motives were manifested in savings deposits. *General Theory of Employment, Interest and Money* (London: Macmillan Co., 1961), p. 195.

We then need to add a household cash demand function

$$m_h = m_h(i) \tag{11}$$

where i is the money rate of interest; and a firm cash demand function,

$$m_f = m_f(i) \tag{12}$$

where i is the money rate of interest, equal to

$$i = r + \pi \tag{13}$$

where π is the rate of inflation, and

$$r = \frac{\partial x}{\partial k_f}(m_f) = r(m_f) \tag{14}$$

is the marginal product of capital, assumed to be a positive function of the stock of real balances held by firms. The system is completed by the equilibrium connection between the rate of monetary expansion and the rate of inflation

$$\rho = \pi \tag{15}$$

in this case where we are abstracting from growth.

A geometric representation of the system can be developed by plotting real balances on the abscissa and rates of change and interest rates on the ordinate. Let us add household and firm cash balances using equations (11) and (12) to get

$$m = m_h + m_f = \Lambda(i) \tag{16}$$

and plot the result as the *ii* schedule in Figure 5-5; it has a negative slope. And let us plot *rr* as the graphic delineation of equation (14); it has a positive slope. Then in the absence of monetary expansion (meaning that the equilibrium rate of inflation is zero) the equilibrium of the system will be decided by the division of cash balances between firms and households. If we draw *ff* as the schedule representing the firms' demand-for-money function [equation (12)] the equilibrium interest rate is established by the intersection of *ff* with *rr* at the point Q. Then RS is the equilibrium stock of real balances held by the community, which is divided between households and firms in the amounts QS and RQ. The equilibrium real and money interest rate is OR.

Now let us consider inflation at the rate $\pi = \rho_1 = UN$. This introduces a gap between real and money rates of interest, driving a wedge between *ff*, a function of the money interest rate, and *rr*, a function of the real interest rate. If UN represents the rate of monetary expansion, real money balances will fall by ZS to TV in the economy as a whole and LQ will be that part of the reduction in the holdings of firms. The real

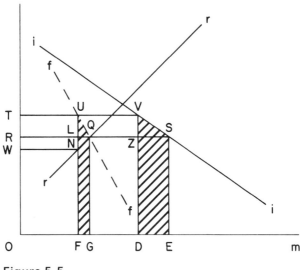

Figure 5-5

rate of interest thus falls to OW, the decline being greater the larger is the elasticity of firms' cash balances compared to the elasticity of demand for money balances in the economy as a whole.

The conclusions of this analysis thus far do not vitiate the more aggregative analysis of the preceding chapters except insofar as they introduce richer possibilities for interpreting the adaptation of real and money rates of interest to inflation. It is easy to see that if the demand for money on the part of households increases, the stock of real money balances in the community as a whole will increase, but there will be no alteration in the real and money rates of interest in the economy as a whole. This is the major difference between the two-sector and one-sector models, and it arises because of the assumption we have made that the real rate of interest is dominated by the money holdings of firms. An increase in real household cash can be generated for the economy as a whole by a general (once-for-all) deflation without subtracting from the equilibrium quantity of cash held by firms.[2]

Before we conclude this part of our analysis it may be useful to present the changes that occur in more precise mathematical form. The consumption potential of the economy could be plotted on a graph in which the liquidity services and output are measured on the coordinates. It is clear from the equation system that the transformation schedule which

2. During the process of adjustment, of course, firms will suffer deficits and households surpluses which will alter equity values that capitalize the forced savings imposed on firms; this effect is analogous to the seigniorage redistribution effects studied in international trade. For a discussion see chapter 15.

results from a fixed quantity of real balances would be convex, as may be
seen directly from equations (9) and (10) when real money balances are
taken as given. There will be a different consumption-potential schedule
for every level of real balances. However, the level of real balances is
uniquely defined by the rate of interest, as may be seen from equations
(11) and (12) or, better, equation (16); the money rate of interest is the
sum of the real rate and the rate of inflation; the rate of inflation is given
by the rate of money expansion; and the real rate is a function of the stock
of cash balances held by firms. Thus the transformation curve would be
uniquely defined for any given rate of monetary expansion. The equations
of it are readily put in the parametric form by the following procedure:

$$l = l[m_h(i)] = l[m_h(r(m_f) + \rho)] = \psi(m_f; \rho) \tag{17}$$

$$x = x[m_f(i)] = x[m_f(r(m_f) + \rho)] = \psi(m_f; \rho) \tag{18}$$

To find the output effects of changing the rate of monetary expansion we
can differentiate to get

$$dl = \frac{\partial l}{\partial m_h} \cdot \frac{\partial m_h}{\partial i} \left(\frac{\partial r}{\partial m_f} dm_f + d\rho \right) \tag{19}$$

$$dx = \frac{\partial x}{\partial m_f} \cdot \frac{\partial m_f}{\partial i} \left(\frac{\partial r}{\partial m_f} dm_f + d\rho \right) \tag{20}$$

from which dm_f can be eliminated by using equation (10), establishing
a direct link between changes in x and l and changes in the rate of monetary
expansion:

$$\frac{dx}{d\rho} = \frac{\dfrac{\partial x}{\partial m_f} \cdot \dfrac{\partial m_f}{\partial i}}{1 - \dfrac{\partial m_f}{\partial i} \cdot \dfrac{\partial r}{\partial m_f}} \tag{21}$$

$$\frac{dl}{d\rho} = \frac{\partial l}{\partial m_h} \cdot \frac{\partial m_h}{\partial i} \left[\frac{\dfrac{\partial r}{\partial m_f} \cdot \dfrac{\partial m_f}{\partial i}}{1 - \dfrac{\partial m_f}{\partial i} \cdot \dfrac{\partial r}{\partial m_f}} \right] \tag{22}$$

Now we know the following signs:

$$\frac{\partial x}{\partial m_f} > 0; \quad \frac{\partial l}{\partial m_h} > 0; \quad \frac{\partial m_f}{\partial i} < 0; \quad \frac{\partial m_h}{\partial i} < 0; \quad \frac{\partial r}{\partial m_f} > 0$$

and this permits the deduction

$$\frac{dx}{d\rho} < 0 \tag{23}$$

and also

$$\frac{dl}{d\rho} < 0 \qquad\qquad (24)$$

as is readily seen by expanding the term on the right of equation (22). Thus, inflation causes a reduction in the output of both commodity and liquidity services. Cash intensities in both the firm and household sectors decline. The value of the loss of output in the firm sector is given in Figure 5-5 by the area $FUQG$, and for the economy as a whole by $DVSE$. But no fundamental change in principle beyond the expected increase in the complexity and richness of the conclusions has been made by introducing the complications of a two-sector model.

chapter 6

inflation, financial intensity, and maximum growth

We now want to probe more deeply into the problems discussed in the preceding chapters. This chapter attempts to compute the growth-maximizing rate of inflationary finance, taking into account the fact that changes in the ratio of money and capital will affect the productivity of capital. It makes some rough estimates about empirical magnitudes, but abstracts from the wealth-saving effect considered in chapter 3 and special hoarding effects analyzed in chapter 5.

Our purpose here is to analyze the conditions of monetary equilibrium in an economy in which the government finances expenditure by money creation. The first section assumes that newly created money is used to finance current expenditure and considers the question of the maximum tax on cash balances. The second part allows for government-financed additions to the rate of capital formation and the third section considers the conditions under which growth is maximized.

CONTRAST BETWEEN SIMPLE MONETARY EXPANSION AND INFLATIONARY FINANCE

We have already analyzed elsewhere the case of simple monetary expansion. Our first task is to contrast the results obtained in that analysis with those from cases where the newly created money is used to buy goods. Whereas in the previous analysis we assumed a per capita subsidy, in this analysis the community has to earn its additional balances by real saving in excess of investment.

Consider a situation where, in the absence of growth, the government finances current expenditure by money creation. The deficit financing will result in a rate of inflation equal to the rate of monetary expansion. Suppose the latter is equal to $AB = DC$. This rate of inflation creates a discrepancy between the money and real rates of interest equal to the inflation rate and establishes w_1 as the equilibrium money-capital ratio corresponding to that rate of money creation. The resources obtained by the government (as a fraction of the capital stock) are the area of the rectangle $ABCD$, which is simply the product of the rate of inflation (or monetary expansion) and the new money-capital ratio.

It is helpful to think of the process in two phases.[1] First, the authorities "announce" a given rate of monetary expansion. The community interprets the announcement as a signal that prices will rise at a given rate equal to the rate of monetary expansion. This renders the community's prior division of its wealth between money and capital now inappropriate because the real cost of holding cash relative to goods has been increased to the extent of the rate of inflation. They will now want to substitute goods for cash, reduce money holdings, and increase capital holdings. But the stock of capital at any moment of time is given, so the attempt to convert money into capital results only in an increase in the price of goods. Thus, the real value of cash balances is diminished, and the actual ratio of real money and capital is lowered. The lower money-capital ratio in turn reduces the marginal productivity of capital and the real rate of interest. The mere anticipation of inflation thus results in actual price increases and a lower rate of interest. In Figure 6-1 the anticipation of inflation at the rate CD lowers the equilibrium money-capital ratio from w_0 to w_1.

The second phase concerns the actual effects of the monetary expansion and the inflation. The inflation rate measures the speed at which existing cash balances are being depreciated, and the product of this rate and the actual holdings of real balances measures the reduction in the community's consumption that is required to maintain real balances constant at the lower level. This forced saving is analogous to a tax or a depreciation allowance.

The real value of government spending is $1/P(dM/dt)$, and the tax

1. See Martin Bailey, "Welfare Cost of Inflationary Finance," *Journal of Political Economy* 66 (Apr. 1956) and *National Income and the Price Level* (New York: McGraw-Hill Book Co., 1962), pp. 51–52 for a lucid description of the distinction between the effects of the portfolio adjustment due to the *expectation* of inflation and those due to the actual inflation itself.

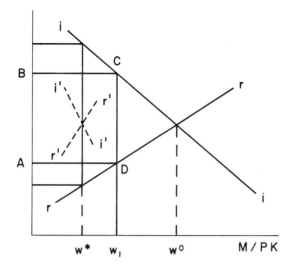

Figure 6-1

on cash balances is $(M/P)(\dot{P}/P)$. That these two are necessarily equal is evident from the equation

$$\frac{d\frac{M/P}{K}}{dt} \equiv \frac{1}{K}\left[\frac{\dot{M}}{P} - \frac{M}{P}\frac{\dot{P}}{P}\right] = 0 \tag{1}$$

which is valid when K, the capital stock, is constant. Both parts of the expression in equation (1) are equivalent to the area $ABCD$ in Figure 6-1.

Let us now consider the differences between the situation portrayed in Figure 6-1 and that which would arise from a "simple" expansion of the quantity of money along the lines considered previously.

The money-capital ratio will be as before, but the equilibrium level of both money and capital will be higher in the case of deficit finance than in the case of simple money expansion, under the assumption that the community saves to attain a given level of wealth. In the case of deficit finance part of the private income of the community is acquired by the government. Given that wealth is the capitalized value of private disposable income, additional accumulation of capital is required to achieve the same level of wealth, while considerations of portfolio balance will ensure a higher level of real money balances also. Thus money and physical capital holdings will both be higher after the new stationary state equilibrium has been attained.

MAXIMUM PROCEEDS

The money-capital ratio at which the government maximizes the proceeds of the tax on cash balances is the ratio at which the area enclosed by corresponding points on *ii*, *rr*, and the ordinate is a maximum. This is determined by the intersection of curves "marginal" to *ii* and *rr*, i.e., the curves *i'i'* and *r'r'*. If, as in Figure 6-1 *ii* and *rr* are straight lines, the maximum is at the point where $w^* = \frac{1}{2}w_0$, i.e., proceeds from the "inflation tax" are maximized when the money-capital ratio has been cut in half. The corresponding inflation rate is then the product of this new money capital ratio and the sum of the slopes of *ii* and *rr*, or

$$\pi = \frac{1}{2}\gamma w_0 \tag{2}$$

where γ is the sum of the slopes of *ii* and *rr*. If, for example, an additional inflation rate of 1 percent would reduce the ratio of money to capital by one percentage point, then $\gamma = 1$, and the revenue-maximizing rate of inflation is one-half the noninflationary money-capital ratio. Assuming that a typical value of the money-capital ratio is one-tenth, as it would be if, say, the capital-output ratio were 2.5 and velocity were 4 under conditions of no inflation, then the rate of inflation at which budget proceeds are maximized by inflationary finance is 5 percent.

INFLATIONARY FINANCE AND GROWTH

To analyze deficit financing for purposes of growth it will be helpful to rewrite the system of equations. First, there is the Fisher relation between inflation and the difference between money and real interest:

$$\pi = i(w) - r(w). \tag{3}$$

Second, there is the quantity theory relation between inflation, growth, and money creation necessary if the money-capital ratio is to be an equilibrium ratio:

$$\rho = \lambda + \pi \tag{4}$$

where ρ is the rate of money expansion, λ is the rate of growth, and π is the rate of inflation. Finally, there is the relation between growth and monetary expansion,

$$\lambda = \frac{\dot{K}}{K} = \frac{G}{PK} = \frac{\dot{M}}{PK} = \frac{\dot{M}}{M} \cdot \frac{M}{PK} = w\rho \tag{5}$$

which assumes that there is no net private saving or investment. The three equations form a complete system with one degree of freedom. Given either λ, π, or ρ, all the remaining variables are completely determined.

The system can be reduced to two equations in π, λ, and w by eliminating ρ from (4) and (5). The combined result of (4) and (5) is then:

$$\pi = \left(\frac{1}{w} - 1\right)\lambda \qquad (6)$$

It is then possible to write the growth rate, λ, as a function solely of the money-capital ratio, w, by equating the right side of equation (6) with the right side of equation (3). After a little manipulation this gives

$$\lambda = \frac{w}{1 - w}\left[i(w) - r(w)\right] \qquad (7)$$

from which, as will be shown, the growth-maximizing rate of inflation associated with the inflationary process can be determined.

First, however, let us represent the system on another diagram. In Figure 6-2, the ii and rr curves are defined as in Figure 6-1, and our problem is to investigate the rate of deficit financing leading to the money-capital ratio w. The implied rate of inflation is LM, and this gives the rate at which cash balances are being taxed. If the tax proceeds were used for current government expenditures that would be the end of the story.

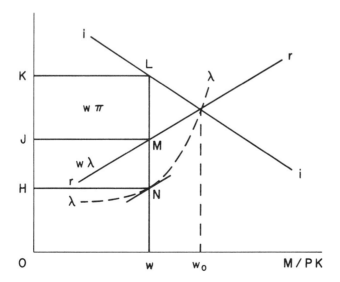

Figure 6-2

The fact that the government spending is used to augment the capital stock, however, introduces a new element into the process. The growth rate induced by the pure tax on cash balances is simply the area of the rectangle $JKLM$; this can be seen by noting that this area is $\pi w = \pi(M/P)/K$ where the numerator is the proceeds of the tax, used to increase the capital stock, and the denominator is the capital stock itself. But this growth rate $JKLM$ itself requires an increase in real cash balances for the money-capital ratio to be maintained. The tax proceeds add to growth, but they also add to the base of the tax, which in turn increases growth, the base of the tax, and so on.

The infinite series, the sum of which gives the growth rate, is

$$\lambda = w\pi(1 + w + w^2 + w^3 + \cdots) = \pi\,\frac{w}{1-w} \tag{8}$$

provided $w < 1$, as it will be in every conceivable case.

In the diagram the sum of the infinite series is MN, where $MN/LM = w/(1-w)$, and this is equal to the rate of growth. But the rate of growth is also represented by the area $HKLN$ since this area is the product of the money-capital ratio and the sum of the inflation rate (LM) and the growth rate (MN).

In the diagram there is a point like N corresponding to any given rate of deficit financing, and the locus of such points traces out the $\lambda\lambda$ curve, the vertical distance between $\lambda\lambda$ and rr tracing out the rate of growth induced by the deficit financing corresponding to the indicated money-capital ratio. The curve clearly passes through Q, since at Q there is no deficit financing or growth, and the distance between $\lambda\lambda$ and rr is zero at that point. The growth distance increases as the money-capital ratio is reduced from Q up to a maximum point, after which the growth distance declines. The vertical distance simply traces out equation (7).

GROWTH MAXIMIZATION

To find the conditions under which growth is maximized by deficit financing, equation (7) can be differentiated with respect to w and the result set equal to zero. The result gives the money-capital ratio at which growth is maximized:

$$w^* = 1 - (1 - w_0)^{\frac{1}{2}}, \tag{9}$$

again on the assumption that the ii and rr schedules can be approximated by straight lines in the relevant range of the curves; in equation (9) w^* is the growth-maximizing w, and w_0 is the money-capital ratio corresponding to zero inflation. It then follows that the rate of inflation associated with the growth-maximizing deficit financing is

$$\pi^* = \gamma[w_0 - 1 + (1 - w_0)^{\frac{1}{2}}] \qquad (10)$$

where γ is the sum of the slopes of rr and ii in absolute terms. The corresponding maximum growth rate is

$$\lambda^* = \gamma[(1 - w_0)^{\frac{1}{2}} - 1]^2. \qquad (11)$$

In the diagram these values are determined by the point on $\lambda\lambda$ where the slope is parallel to the slope of rr. The situation depicted at N with the inflation rate LM and the growth rate MN is in fact the growth-maximizing configuration.

It is possible to establish an outside limit on the growth-maximizing money-capital ratio (w^*) by showing first, on the assumption of linearity of rr and ii, that w^* is greater than one-half w_0, the inflationless money-capital ratio. This follows at once, given that w_0 is a positive fraction, because $w^* > \frac{1}{2}w_0$ is, from (9), equivalent to

$$1 - (1 - w_0)^{\frac{1}{2}} > \frac{1}{2}w_0 \qquad (12)$$

which has to be true. This simple result can be related to our earlier conclusion that the money-capital ratio at which deficit financing for current expenditure is maximized is equal to one-half the inflationless money-capital ratio; but (12) proves that if a government carried inflationary finance for purposes of development this far, it would have gone past the point of growth maximization. This is easily seen also by reference to Figure 6-2; maximizing the area enclosed between ii and rr will result in a lower money-capital ratio and a higher inflation rate than maximizing the area between ii and $\lambda\lambda$.

PRIVATE SAVING

Until now we have ignored private saving except for our earlier consideration of the wealth effect. Let us now assume that a given fraction of income, s, is saved. Let ϕ represent the product of capital. Then $\gamma = \Omega\phi$ expresses the relation between real interest and the average product of capital, where Ω is the share of real interest in income. Private growth is $s\phi$, so that total growth is

$$\lambda = \frac{sr(w)}{\Omega} + w\rho, \qquad (13)$$

which replaces equation (5) in the system. The solution for λ in terms of w is then

$$\lambda = \frac{w}{1-w}[i(w) - r(w)] + \frac{sr(w)}{(1-w)\Omega}, \tag{14}$$

differentiation of which yields

$$\frac{d\lambda}{dw} = \frac{w}{1-w}[i'(w) - r'(w)] + \frac{i(w) - r(w)}{(1-w)^2} + \frac{s}{\Omega}\frac{(1-w)r'(w) + r(w)}{(1-w)^2} \tag{15}$$

Growth is maximized when $d\lambda/dw = 0$. Assuming linearity of $r(w)$ and $i(w)$, setting (15) equal to zero gives

$$w^{**} = 1 - \left(1 - w_0 - \frac{sr'}{\Omega}\frac{1+\bar{w}}{\gamma}\right)^{\frac{1}{2}} \tag{16}$$

where w^{**} is the money-capital ratio at maximum growth, r' is the slope of rr, and $\bar{w}$ is the value, defined positive, of w at which r would in principle be zero. The previous optimum w^* from equation (9) is a special case of w^{**} where $s = 0$.

The fact of private saving and investment reduces some of the advantages of deficit financing. It can be shown that the growth-maximizing money-capital ratio may be considerably larger than one-half the inflationless value, which means that the inflation rate associated with maximum output will be smaller. In that case the inflationary finance, while initially increasing public growth, tends to reduce private growth because the inflation lowers the productivity of capital through reducing the money-capital ratio, establishing the conclusion that a country with no private saving and investment may stand to gain by a program of deficit financing in contrast to a country in which there is already a certain amount of private saving and investment. The greater the private savings investment the lower will be the inflation rate associated with maximum growth.

For these reasons any inflation rate sufficient to lower the ratio of money to capital to as much as half its inflationless value would certainly be excessive. If w_0 is one-tenth, then any deficit financing program which pushed the money-capital ratio down one-twentieth would clearly be excessive, assuming as before linearity of rr and ii within the relative range. Unfortunately this is not sufficient to determine the associated inflation rate unless the sum of the slopes of rr and ii is known. Empirical estimates of this sum, γ, have not been made.

For the sake of illustration, however, let us ponder some possible, if not likely, magnitudes. Suppose that from an initial $w_0 = \frac{1}{10}$, an increase in the money rate of interest from 5 percent to 10 percent would cause people to want to reduce their portfolio rate to $\frac{7}{100}$. This is equivalent to assuming, over this range, that the elasticity of ii is $[(10-5)/5]/[(10-7)/100]$

$= 33\frac{1}{3}$, where the elasticity is defined so as to have, normally, a positive value, and the slope of ii is $(10 - 5)/(10 - 7) = \frac{5}{3}$ in absolute value. Suppose also that the same reduction in w from $\frac{1}{10}$ to $\frac{7}{100}$ would lower the real rate of interest by 1 percent, giving a slope of rr equal to $\frac{1}{3}$. In that case the sum of the slopes, γ, would be equal to 2.

On this assumption the inflation rate associated with maximum growth is 10 percent. This can be derived by first calculating the money-capital ratio from equation (11) and substituting $w_0 = \frac{1}{10}$:

$$w^* = 1 - (1 - \tfrac{1}{10})^{\frac{1}{2}} = .0513,$$

which is, as it must be, larger than $\frac{1}{2} w_0$. Substituting the result into

$$\pi^* = \gamma(w_0 - w^*)$$

gives

$$\pi^* = 2(.1 - .0513) = 9.7 \text{ percent.}$$

The result could be got directly from equation (10). Associated with this inflation rate will be the maximum growth rate, obtained by substituting the values for w_0 and γ into the formula for maximum growth (10):

$$\lambda^* - 2[(1 - \tfrac{1}{10})^{\frac{1}{2}} - 1]^2 = 0.53 \text{ percent.}$$

Under these circumstances, therefore, the maximum annual growth rate obtained through deficit financing is slightly over one-half of one percent, and with that growth rate will be associated an annual inflation rate of about 10 percent.

chapter 7

the problem of stopping inflation

This chapter relaxes the assumptions of previous chapters that inflation rates are perfectly foreseen and that asset holders are in equilibrium, and it raises the problem of stopping inflation. It takes into account the lags in the adjustment of desired to actual cash balances and in the adaptation of expectations, explores cyclical tendencies imparted by the inflationary processes, and considers the policy problem of the rate at which inflation should be decelerated. It represents an application of control theory to the problem of inflation.

THE DYNAMICS OF ADJUSTMENT

The monetary authorities determine the nominal quantity of money, but the community itself determines, through decisions to hold or spend money, the real value of the money in existence and with given output, income velocity. When the ratio of actual income (or, more exactly,

Adapted from "Growth, Stability and Inflationary Finance," *Journal of Political Economy* 73 (Apr. 1965): 97–109, by permission of The University of Chicago Press. Copyright 1965 by the University of Chicago.

transactions) to cash, that is, income velocity, is greater than the desired ratio or when real cash balances are below the desired level, spending and the rate of inflation can be assumed to decrease, lowering actual velocity; and, when velocity is less than the desired velocity, spending, the rate of inflation, and actual velocity are raised. Expressing these changes in terms of the logarithms (indexes) of desired and actual velocity and assuming that the adjustment process is linear, we have

$$\alpha \frac{dW}{dt} = W^* - W, \tag{1}$$

where W and W^* denote, respectively, the logarithms of actual and desired velocity and α is a measure of the sluggishness of the reaction. As α becomes smaller, the speed of the adjustment becomes larger.

To introduce the hypothesis of "adaptive expectations" used in prior studies by Philip Cagan and Maurice Allais, through which expectations are revised upward or downward according to whether previous predictions were too low or too high, we assume

$$\beta \frac{d\pi'}{dt} = \pi - \pi', \tag{2}$$

where π' and π are, respectively, the expected and the actual inflation rates and β is the reaction delay in the adjustment of expectations. When β is very low, say zero, the adjustment is instantaneous, and the expected inflation rate is equal to the actual inflation rate.

The system is completed by expressions for the desired level of velocity and the equation of exchange. Assuming that the logarithm of velocity is a linear function of the expected rate of inflation we have[1]

$$W^* = a\pi' + b. \tag{3}$$

Also, from the equation of exchange, assuming no growth, we have

$$\frac{dW}{dt} = \pi - \rho, \tag{4}$$

where, as before, ρ is the rate of monetary expansion, assumed to be given.

---

1. Except that the logarithm of velocity instead of the logarithm of real balances is used, this function is of the same form as that used by Cagan "Monetary Dynamics of Hyperinflation," in *Studies in the Quantity Theory of Money*, ed. M. Friedman (Chicago: University of Chicago Press, 1968), pp. 25–117.

STABILITY OF THE SYSTEM

If W^* is eliminated from the four equations (1)—(4) by substituting equation (3) into equation (1), the system reduces to three differential equations which can be compactly expressed in the following matrix form:

$$\begin{bmatrix} \alpha\delta + 1 & 0 & -a \\ \delta & -1 & 0 \\ 0 & -1 & \beta\delta + 1 \end{bmatrix} \begin{pmatrix} W \\ \pi \\ \pi' \end{pmatrix} = \begin{pmatrix} b \\ -\rho \\ 0 \end{pmatrix}, \tag{5}$$

where $\delta \equiv d/dt$ is the differential operator. The stability of the system depends on whether the roots of the characteristic equation, formed by setting the determinant of the coefficient matrix of the system of equations (5) equal to zero, have negative or positive real parts. When the characteristic equation is expanded in powers of δ, we have

$$\alpha\beta\delta^2 + (\alpha + \beta - a)\delta + 1 = 0, \tag{6}$$

so that

$$\delta_1, \delta_2 = \frac{-(\alpha + \beta - a) \pm \sqrt{[(\alpha + \beta - a)^2 - 4\alpha\beta]}}{2\alpha\beta}. \tag{7}$$

Clearly, the roots in (7) will have negative real parts if and only if

$$\alpha + \beta - a > 0, \tag{8}$$

and this is the stability condition.[2] The system is stable only if the sum of the delays in adjusting expectations and velocity exceeds the logarithmic slope of the velocity function.

A further characteristic of the system is evident from equation (7). The system will have real or complex roots depending upon whether the discriminant is positive or negative, that is, depending upon whether

$$(\alpha + \beta - a)^2 \gtrless 4\alpha\beta. \tag{9}$$

This condition is more stringent than equation (8), so that if the system is close to the borderline of stability it must oscillate.

There is a sense in which the two delays, α and β, are "confounded" in the system. Interchanging α and β does not affect the stability condition equation (8) or the criterion of real or complex roots equation (9) in any

2. Cagan's stability condition, which is derived by different methods (op. cit, pp. 64–73), is essentially $\beta > a$ (in my terminology) because he assumed that $1/\alpha$, the speed of adjustment of cash balances, is instantaneous. Later he relaxes this assumption (pp. 73–77) without making any adjustment in his stability condition.

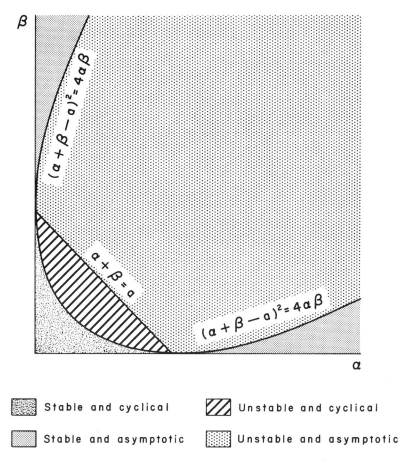

Figure 7-1 Delays in adjusting velocity and expectations are α and β. The straight line separates stable from unstable combinations and parabola separates cyclical from asymptotic solutions. If the system is stable and α and β are similar in magnitude, rate of inflation and velocity will oscillate in their approach to equilibrium.

way. In the stability chart (Figure 7-1) which plots the borderline conditions $\alpha + \beta = a$ (separating stable from unstable regions) and $(\alpha + \beta - a)^2 = 4\alpha\beta$ (separating complex from real solutions), reversing the axes has no effect on the location of the various zones, since both curves are symmetrical with respect to α and β.

There is, nevertheless, one way of inferring, by observation, the relative orders of magnitude of α and β. For if the delays are greatly dissimilar there will be no tendency for the system to reach equilibrium in an oscillatory manner, whereas if the delays are of the same order of magnitude, the system, if it is stable, must oscillate. From observation about the nature of the inflationary process in the real world—whether or not it tends to oscillate—we can infer the relative dimensions of the two lags.[3]

In order to examine the economic meaning of the stability condition it is instructive to take the special case where the system is on the borderline between stability and instability, that is, where $\alpha + \beta = \alpha$. If π' is eliminated from (5) to get an expression for the system in the two variables, π and W, we get

$$\alpha\beta \frac{d\pi}{dt} = -(\alpha + \beta - a)\pi - W + (\alpha + \beta)\rho + b, \qquad (10)$$

and

$$\frac{dW}{dt} = \pi - \rho. \qquad (11)$$

Equation (10) shows that π is constant when

$$W = (\alpha + \beta)\rho + b - (\alpha + \beta - a)\pi \qquad (12)$$

and (11) shows that W is constant when

$$\pi = \rho. \qquad (13)$$

Figure 7-2 plots equation (12) as the line LL and equation (13) as the line RR on the assumption that $\alpha + \beta - a = 0$. In that case LL is horizontal and RR is vertical. At values of π greater than ρ (to the right of RR), W is rising, and at values of π less than ρ (to the left of RR), W is falling. Similarly, at values of W greater or less than $(\alpha + \beta)\rho + b$ (above or below LL), π is, respectively, falling or rising. These dynamic forces govern the paths of W and π over time.

In the case of neutral stability under consideration, it is readily shown that, in disequilibrium, W and π move in an elliptical path. This can be seen by solving equations (10) and (11) and eliminating t. Since the roots are imaginary, the solutions are

$$W - a\rho - b = A \cos ht + B \sin ht, \qquad (14)$$

3. Cagan argues that it is empirically impossible to disentangle the two "lags" (op cit., pp. 75–76), but that "it hardly seems possible that the lag in the balances could be more than a fraction as long as the lag in expectations." However, this carries with it the empirical implication, of which Cagan was unaware, that the approach to equilibrium is not oscillatory, a result which does not seem to accord with many inflations, including the ones Cagan studied.

Nevertheless, the source of the apparent cyclicity in many inflations could arise from cycles in the rate of monetary expansion, a cause which would not invalidate Cagan's intuitive hunch about the relative size of the lags.

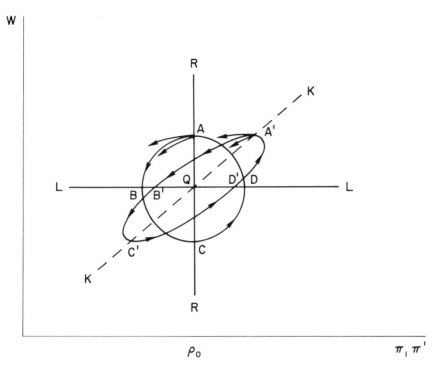

Figure 7-2   In the borderline case where LL is horizontal, which applies when $\alpha + \beta = a$, variables oscillate around equilibrium, W and π in a circle, W and π' in an ellipse. When $\alpha + \beta < a$, LL has a positive slope and the system is unstable. When $\alpha + \beta > a$, LL has a negative slope and the system is stable.

and

$$\pi - \rho = hB \cos ht - hA \sin ht, \tag{15}$$

where $h = 1/\sqrt{(\alpha\beta)}$ and A and B depend only on initial conditions. Solving for $\cos ht$ and $\sin ht$ in equations (14) and (15) and eliminating them by means of the trigonometric identity, $\sin^2 + \cos^2 = 1$, gives

$$(W - a\rho - b)^2 + \alpha\beta(\pi - \rho)^2 = A^2 + B^2, \tag{16}$$

which describes an ellipse about the equilibrium point.

An oscillation in W and π must also involve a sympathetic oscillation in π'. The solution of the system of equations (5) for π', again on the assumption that $\alpha + \beta = a$, is

$$\pi' - \rho = \frac{A + \alpha hB}{a} \cos ht + \frac{B - \alpha hA}{a} \sin ht. \tag{17}$$

Following the same procedure as before, we find the paths in $W\pi'$ space and $\pi\pi'$ space as

$$\frac{\alpha + \beta}{\alpha}(W - a\rho - b)^2$$

$$-\frac{2\beta(\alpha + \beta)}{\alpha}(W - a\rho - b)(\pi' - \rho) + \frac{\beta(\alpha + \beta)^2}{\alpha}(\pi' - \rho) = A^2 + B^2, \tag{18}$$

and

$$\alpha(\alpha + \beta)(\pi - \rho)^2 - 2\alpha(\alpha + \beta)(\pi - \rho)(\pi' - \rho)$$

$$+ (\alpha + \beta)^2(\pi' - \rho)^2 = A^2 + B^2, \tag{19}$$

which are also ellipses centered around the equilibrium point.

The ellipsoidal motion of the three variables, W, π, and π', can be seen by referring again[4] to Figure 7-2. The line KK plots the desired W against π', the expected inflation rate, and can be interpreted as the line in $W\pi'$ space along which there is no tendency for velocity to change. Now consider a point such as A, where $\pi = \rho$, but where W is above equilibrium. At this point W will be constant but π will be falling. Since W is constant, the point A must correspond, in $W-\pi'$ space, to the point A' because, for W to be constant, both $\pi = \rho$ and $W = W^*$ are necessary and so A' must be on KK. Then as the $W-\pi$ orbit travels the path $ABCD$, the $W-\pi'$ orbit travels the elliptical path $A'B'C'D'$. Expected inflation, which starts out (at A') greater than actual inflation, eventually slows down to actual inflation (at B') and then follows it until it again catches up (at D').

The importance of the stability condition can now be perceived. In the borderline case LL is flat. But if *either* α or β is slightly increased, LL takes on a negative slope. In the path from A to B, the forces pulling π below the equilibrium level are slightly reduced, and the orbit moves inside the $W\pi$ orbit as the inner arrow from A indicates, and eventually moves to the equilibrium in a convergent spiral. The same is true for the $W-\pi'$ orbit as the forces working horizontally on the movement of π' are weakened; the arrow from A' moves inside the ellipse, and the path converges. Exactly the opposite occurs when α or β are slightly decreased; the system then diverges as indicated by the outer arrows from A and A'.

---

4. The eccentricities of the ellipses depend partly on time units since π has a time dimension whereas W is dimensionless. Note that a change in time units has an equal effect on α, β, and a, which are all measured in (say) months, as it must, of course, if the stability conditions are to be invariant with respect to arbitrary choices of time units. The $W\pi$ orbit in Figure 7-2 need not necessarily be a circle, and will not be unless $\alpha\beta = 1$.

STOPPING INFLATION

The discussion provides a framework for analyzing alternative methods for stopping inflation. The problem of stopping inflation involves changes in the rate of monetary expansion. What time path should the money supply follow during transition from a given inflation rate to price stability?[5]

It is evident at the outset that ending monetary expansion abruptly is not likely to be the correct policy. Velocity has to fall as inflation is reduced, and if monetary expansion is suddenly cut off, money income must fall.

The implications of ending monetary expansion abruptly are illustrated in Figure 7-3. From an initial point of inflationary equilibrium at Q corresponding to the rate of monetary expansion, ρ_0, stopping the monetary expansion abruptly results in the new equilibrium, S, with a lower velocity. But in moving from Q to S, velocity must first rise, as people's cash balances become squeezed, until a point like R is reached. After R there is a period of deflation and then either an asymptotic movement to S, or, as in the diagram, a cyclical movement through T, depending on the nature of the characteristic roots of the underlying dynamic system. In any event the path from R to S involves a proportionate fall in the price level equal to the percentage drop in velocity between Q and S.

An alternative method is to reduce the rate of monetary expansion in stages. This is illustrated in Figure 7-3 by the successive movements, first to N and then to S. In this case the extent of the deflation in the final stages will be less and the swings in velocity smaller. It is nevertheless doubtful whether a series of smaller adjustments is less painful than one big adjustment.

If *discrete* drops in the rate of monetary expansion are defective, gradual reduction can be considered. One possibility is to reduce the rate of monetary expansion in proportion to the rate of inflation, in accordance with the equation

$$\gamma \frac{d\rho}{dt} = -\pi, \tag{20}$$

where γ is the delay in the process. However, if equation (20) is substituted into the basic system (5) the differential equation in π becomes

$$\alpha\beta\gamma \frac{d^3\pi}{dt^3} + [\alpha\beta + \gamma(\alpha + \beta - a)] \frac{d^2\pi}{dt^2} + \gamma \frac{d\pi}{dt} + \pi = 0, \tag{21}$$

5. Some of the matters discussed in this section have been considered in R. A. Kessel and A. A. Alchian, "Effects of Inflation," *Journal of Political Economy* 70 (Dec. 1962): 521–37.

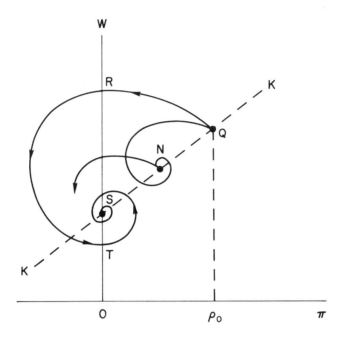

Figure 7-3   If rate of monetary expansion of ρ_0 is suddenly ended, velocity will initially rise and then fall to new
equilibrium at S, but only after price level has declined in
absolute terms. Stopping inflation in stages, illustrated by
moving first to N and then to S, will tend to decrease
amplitude of the swings in velocity and rate of inflation but
will not end them altogether, except in the limiting case
where the reduction in ρ is asymptotic.

which will be stable only if a more stringent condition than equation (8)
is satisfied. Specifically, stability in this case will require that

$$\alpha + \beta - a > 0 \tag{22}$$

The stability condition is the same as before despite the fact that we have
introduced new complexities into the system.

   To achieve perfect results in the sense of going at once to a stable
price level[6] we can set $\pi = 0$ in the basic system [equation (5) of the
previous chapter], repeated here for convenience:

6. I am indebted to Martin Bailey for this suggestion, made at a 1963 seminar at the
IMF where this paper was first presented.

$$\begin{bmatrix} a\delta + 1 & 0 & -a \\ \delta & -1 & 0 \\ 0 & -1 & \beta\delta + 1 \end{bmatrix} \begin{pmatrix} W \\ \pi \\ \pi' \end{pmatrix} = \begin{pmatrix} b \\ -\rho \\ 0 \end{pmatrix},$$

and find the solution for ρ. The result is

$$\rho = Ae^{-(1/a)t} + Be^{-(1/\beta)t} \tag{23}$$

for $a \neq \beta$, where A and B depend on the prestabilization rate of monetary expansion, the delays in adjustment, and the initial discrepancy of the variables from their inflationary equilibrium values.

Application of this rule for reducing the rate of monetary expansion stops inflation without causing deflation. Although prices are stabilized, the monetary expansion continues at a (declining) rate just sufficient to offset changes in velocity. The interesting result is that even though the underlying system may lead to cycles of rates of inflation, a process of tapering the inflation off gradually can eliminate these cycles. The path indicated by equation (23) is asymptotic, which means that the rate of monetary expansion does not have to reflect potential cycles in order to insure a smooth adjustment to a constant price level. The new equilibrium level of the money supply will be higher than the level at the time of stabilization, and the price level will be constant throughout.

In any actual situation it will not, of course, be possible to establish accurate values for a and β in equation (23), so that the problem of stopping inflation must involve considerable guesswork. Perhaps the safest rule is to abandon the exceedingly delicate goal of precisely stabilizing the price index and planning instead on moving to price stability at a somewhat higher price level. The longer the time required for stabilization, the higher the ultimate price level will be, a factor of relevance in setting new exchange rates. But the opposite danger is more severe. If the monetary expansion is ended too abruptly, the ensuing depression can discredit the entire process.

II

the world economy

chapter 8

monetary theory and the world gold standard

Economic theory and economic policy are mutual complements in the sense that the creation of relevant theory increases the marginal productivity of decision making, while the increasing importance of policy decisions raises the marginal utility of theory. Policy is out of date when a theory more obsolete than necessary is used, and theory is backward when policy makers have to develop ad hoc theories of their own or rely on the luck of intuition. Problems crop up unexpectedly, however, and the mark of a mature science is its ability to contribute solutions quickly. For this purpose a science should have on hand a reservoir of models capable of quick conversion to practical use. Thus it is helpful to have on hand depression models even though the world is in a state of inflation, or growth models even if the world is retrogressing.

Constructing models is the task of the mathematical economist; choosing a model is the task of the economic theorist. After the mathematician establishes the relations, the theorist classifies them and points out their relevance, thus providing a bridge between the deductive activity of the mathematician and the inductive activity of the empiricist. Time is not unlimited, however, so even abstract models which are "goods" when relevant can become "bads" when they distract attention from more relevant intellectual enterprise or turn out to be positively misleading.

This means that we must have criteria for distinguishing good models from bad models.

The economic theorist has two major tools as arbiters of value: one is empirical relevance; the other is axiomatic consistency. Models can be rejected because they fail to meet the two fundamental tests of economic reliability and relevance: conformity to experience (a matter of history and econometrics), and/or conformity to the axioms on which the science is founded. In economics, the unifying core of theory is the axiom of rational self-interest; belief in the relevance of this axiom is the science's sine qua non.

The applied theorist seeks usable theory to adapt to practical problems. Adaptation implies transformation of the theoretical form to suit the problem and specification of the data upon which policy makers have to act. The first activity gives the theoretical form relevance, while the second is an inherent component of the communications transmission mechanism. To take a journey a driver must not only have a car that works, he also needs instructions on how it runs and a road map.

THE THEORETICAL PROBLEM

The subject of this chapter fits between the work of the abstract theorist and the applied theorist. We do not have a gold standard system, or a gold exchange standard, or a dollar standard of the exact kind I am going to analyze. Even if a gold standard system were to be introduced, it would have to be managed by a gold authority empowered to neutralize upsetting disturbances caused by gold hoarding, Russian gold policy, and the South African gold supply. In this sense the first system presented would better inform policy makers of, say, the 1890s than it would the monetary authorities of today. Nor do we have a gold exchange standard or a dollar standard of the simple variety studied here.

The major theoretical problem to be solved in a discussion of the gold standard system is the synthesis of stocks and flows in the markets for capital and money. One of the attributes of gold, in addition to its durability, that has made it such a successful money commodity is the vast holdings of it in relation to annual production, a phenomenon which gives gold its essential money property: its marginal utility declines at a slower rate than the marginal utility of other assets.

At any given moment the world community—composed of central bankers, private hoarders, industrial users, and gold producers—holds the existing stock. The relative prices of gold and commodities or reserve ratios will adjust to ensure equilibrium, placing the *real* price of gold, or the value of gold, at the forefront of any global gold standard analysis. However, the fact that annual production is small in relation to stocks

outstanding does not mean that fluctuations in this rate have an insignificant effect upon the system's equilibrium. The rate of growth of gold
stocks is dimensionally equivalent to the rate of growth of commodities,
and it bears, in growth equilibrium, a definable relation to the rate of
interest. The rate of interest has a direct bearing upon the holding of
stocks of gold and of commodities, and thence upon the real price of gold,
which in turn influences gold production. This means that relatively small
fluctuations in gold production can have substantial effects, through the
route of expectations, upon price levels or upon income and employment.

We shall not go into the complications associated with changes in
real output or controversies connected with the theory of employment.
Rather, we shall bring together the complex general equilibrium interactions between stocks and flows, real and nominal interest rates, expectations, the rate of gold production, and the rate of capital growth; these
need to be fitted into an analytically coherent framework in the institutional
context of the international gold standard. Then we can adapt the model
as necessary to explore the gold exchange standard and the dollar standard.

THE GOLD STANDARD

Assume that the equilibrium of the world economy is dominated by
growth in the production of goods and services on the one hand, and by
the growth of the world's stock of money on the other. In the simplest
case, where the income elasticity of demand for world money is close to
unity, world prices will have a tendency to rise or fall depending on whether
world output is growing at a faster or slower pace than world money.

In order to focus attention on the essential properties of the gold
standard and other systems we shall develop the argument by reference
to a simple diagram (Figure 8-1). We plot on the ordinate the various
interest rates and growth rates and on the abscissa the real value of world
reserves which, in the case of the gold standard, is the value of gold in terms
of commodities.

The equilibrium interest rate and the real gold stock will be determined, in the absence of growth, by the intersection of two schedules, one
specifying the conditions of equilibrium in the market for gold, the other
for goods. The MM curve, the money-balance schedule, relates the values
of real gold balances the world community of nations would wish to hold
at various nominal rates of interest; it is assumed to have a negative slope
because the opportunity cost of holding real gold balances increases with
the rate of interest. The KK curve, which I shall refer to as the capital-
balance schedule, relates the own rate of return on capital goods to the
real value of gold balances; it has a positive slope both because an increase

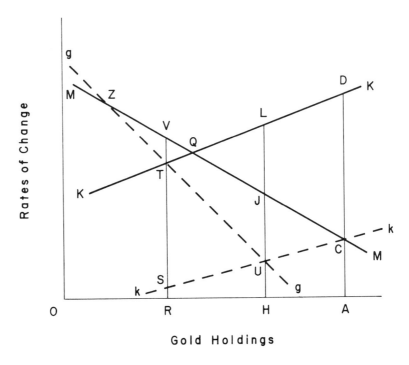

Figure 8-1

in real money balances, in money's role as an instrumental factor, raises the real return to capital, and because money, in its role as a consumer asset, is a component of wealth and thus influences saving.

If we could ignore questions of accumulation, the equilibrium interest rate and level of real gold balances would be established at Q, the point where KK intersects MM.

At reserve levels higher than implied by this equilibrium, the own interest rate on goods would exceed the own interest rate on gold by the vertical gap between KK and MM. Unless the community members expected deflation to an equal degree there would be a tendency to buy goods, bidding up the price level; the opposite would occur if the level of real reserve balances were below the equilibrium. Only at Q would the system be in an equilibrium that corresponded to no expected or actual changes in relative prices.

The facts of accumulation and the production of money, however, mean that expectations of zero price level changes would be viable only by chance. Let us, therefore, take growth explicitly into account. Under the gold standard, the rate of money expansion is an endogenous variable. At any moment, the stock of gold is given, but the rate at which it is changing is influenced by the real price of gold; producers will expand production up to the point where the marginal cost is equal to the price. With increasing opportunity costs gold production will be higher the lower is the world price level, so that there will be a unique rate of gold production corresponding to every given level of real gold balances. This is indicated by the gg schedule, which is derived from the MM line by subtracting from MM the rate of gold production expressed as a proportion of actual reserves. At some sufficiently low real price of gold (high gold price of goods) gold production would be nil, as at the point Z.

If the stock of gold were growing but not the level of non gold output, an inflationary equilibrium would be established at a point where the rate of gold expansion were equal to the rate of inflation. A given rate of inflation will, of course, raise the cost of holding gold balances, and the community will prefer to economize on gold by holding a smaller stock of gold in its portfolio. Thus, the equilibrium will be determined at the point where two conditions are met. First, the rate of monetary expansion must equal the rate of inflation; this is necessary if velocity is to remain constant, as it must in a period of monetary equilibrium. This means that the vertical gap between gg and MM, which is the rate of monetary expansion, must also correspond to the rate of (price) inflation. Second, it means that the vertical gap between MM and KK, which corresponds to the difference between the cost of holding money (the nominal interest rate) and the real interest rate, and therefore the expected rate of inflation, must also equal the actual rate of inflation. Thus, equilibrium would settle at the point T, with the nominal interest rate equal to VR, the real interest rate equal to TR, and both the expected and actual rate of inflation and the rate of monetary expansion equal to VT.

But we must now take growth into account. A positive rate of world monetary expansion would not necessarily imply inflation if the world economy were growing. We have already derived a schedule, gg, representing the rate of gold production. An analogous construction applies to world output. World production is higher, relative to gold production, the higher is the world price level in terms of gold—resources are shifted from gold to goods. Thus, kk is determined by subtracting the rate of growth of output from the KK schedule.

We can now inquire into the nature of the equilibrium that would be established if output, but not gold, were growing. In this instance there would be a steady increase in the demand for money and a corresponding ex ante gap between world income and expenditure that would induce deflationary pressure. Equilibrium could only be established at the point where the real value of gold balances was growing at a rate equal to the rate of growth of world output. Thus, equilibrium would settle at the point where kk intersects MM, yielding a real rate of interest equal to AD, a nominal rate of interest equal to AC, and a rate of growth and deflation equal to DC.

Of course in the normal case both gold and commodities will be expanding, and that will establish an equilibrium at U, where kk and gg intersect one another. At the equilibrium thus established we can make the following identifications, along with illustrative values to depict the nature of the world economy in the late nineteenth century:

LH = real rate of interest = r = 5 percent;
JH = nominal rate of interest = i = 3 percent;
LJ = expected and actual rate of inflation = π = -2 percent;
LU = rate of growth = λ = 4 percent;
JU = rate of gold production = ρ = 2 percent.

THE GOLD EXCHANGE STANDARD AND ITS COLLAPSE

Let us now adapt the apparatus to take into account the modern fact that international reserves are composed of both gold and foreign exchange, which we shall call dollars, and that during the 1950s and 1960s countries relied on dollars for a substantial fraction of their reserve growth.

Figure 8-2 replicates the basic structure of Figure 8-1 except that it places the real value of international reserves on the abscissa, including both gold and dollar holdings. If the world economy had to rely upon gold alone for reserve growth equilibrium would settle at the point U, with deflationary pressure in the world as a whole analogous to that prevailing in the 1880s. Instead, however, dollars supplied in the 1950s an important component of world reserve growth. The U.S. balance of payments deficit has to be introduced into the diagram.

Define the U.S. balance of payments deficit as a percentage of the total level of reserves.[1] Then this percentage, which has the dimension of a logarithmic rate of change, can be introduced directly into Figure 8-2 as a gap between the gg and kk curves. As long as central banks are confident that dollars and gold are convertible into one another, a dollar's worth of reserves supplied in the form of gold and a dollar's worth of reserves supplied in terms of dollars are equivalent from the standpoint of their effect on the equilibrium of the system. Subtract the U.S. deficit, then, from the gg curve to get a curve of total world monetary expansion;

1. For certain purposes, it would be more elegant and appropriate to incorporate the entire U.S. economy into the "rest of the world," as I did in another article [*International Economics* (New York: Macmillan Co., 1968) chap. 20], although this results in certain complications associated with the burden of adjustment (see Ibid., chap. 13, esp. p. 198). Such complications are excluded here.

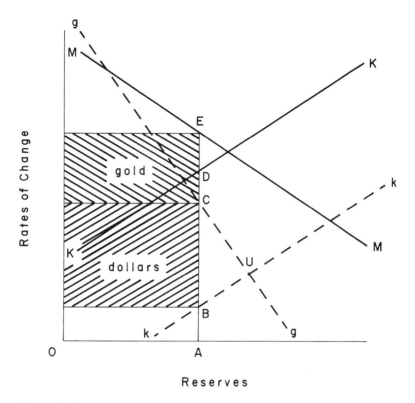

Figure 8-2

the point where such a curve, if drawn, would intersect *KK* would thus establish the equilibrium of the system.

Suppose the U.S. deficit, expressed as a percentage of world reserves, is equal to *CB*. Then the system would settle down to equilibrium with a level of real reserves equal to *OA*. We can then establish the following identifications, more or less applicable to the 1950s, when the gold exchange standard appeared to be viable:

AD = real rate of interest = r = 5 percent;
AE = nominal rate of interest = i = 6 percent;
ED = expected and actual rate of inflation = π = 1 percent;
DB = rate of growth = λ = 4 percent;
EC = rate of gold production = ρ = 2 percent;
BC = rate of dollar expansion = δ = 3 percent.

It is clear from the diagram how the rate of dollar expansion determines the rate of inflation in the world as a whole. The upper and lower shaded areas represent, respectively, the real value of gold production and the real value of the U.S. payments deficit.

The year of 1958, when European currencies became externally convertible, can be regarded as a rough date of the transition of the system. From 1958 to 1968, gold production did not provide any new reserves to the monetary authorities; the modest increase in gold reserves supplied up until 1967 was cancelled by the losses associated with the November 1967 devaluation of sterling and the March 17, 1968, communique isolating official holdings from the private market. There was, however, a redistribution of gold from the U.S. to the rest of the world. The viable gold exchange standard of the 1950s became the unsustainable gold exchange standard of the 1960s. World holdings of foreign exchange increased by about $10 billion over the period.

The equilibrium of the system is illustrated in Figure 8-3, in which we have dropped the gg line since production in this period was not a source of monetary reserves for central banks.

The "equilibrium" in Figure 8-3 represents a transitional phase in

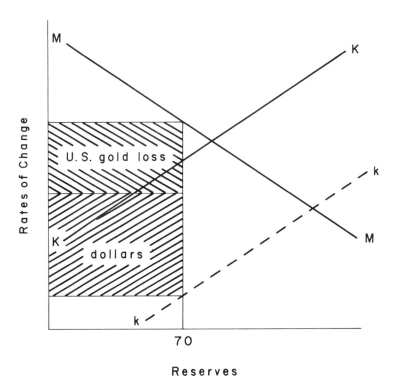

Figure 8-3

the international monetary system. According to the conventions of official accounting, the total shaded area represents the U.S. balance of payments deficit.

It is obvious that the system depicted in Figure 8-3 could not last. It broke down, effectively, in the spring of 1968; in March the leakage of gold from official reserves to private markets was cut off so that the only source of gold loss to the U.S. can arise from foreign central bank conversions. It is probably understood, however, that conversions on any substantial scale would result in a cessation of the privilege.

The same inflationary equilibrium of the system would therefore require an accelerated rate of dollar expansion if reserves in the rest of the world are to continue growing at the same rate as in the 1960s. This might imply magnitudes over the coming years such as the following:

$$r = 4 \text{ percent,}$$
$$i = 6 \text{ percent,}$$
$$\pi = 2 \text{ percent,}$$
$$\lambda = 4 \text{ percent,}$$
$$\text{and } \delta = 6 \text{ percent.}$$

chapter 9

devaluation

This chapter analyzes some of the effects of devaluation in a small country. A country would normally contemplate devaluation only from a position of disequilibrium. For analytical purposes, however, it is convenient to start from a position of equilibrium in order to determine the nature of the disequilibrium that would be created by the devaluation, and then later reverse the process in order to discover the disequilibrium characteristics which render devaluation appropriate.

BASIC ASSUMPTIONS

Assume we are dealing with, initially, a very simple, open economy for which the terms of trade are fixed by international considerations, and assume the foreign currency price of both imports and exports in world markets is fixed.[1] This means that a change in the exchange rate will have the effect of raising the price of both imports and exports to the same extent in the home economy without altering the terms of trade. Assume also that the residents of the country under consideration hold their assets

1. This assumption was introduced into formal analysis by Roland Wilson in his analysis of the transfer problem in the 1930s; it has been used extensively by A. Harberger in his analyses of devaluations in Latin America.

primarily in the form of domestic money and that their basic commodity and production choices rest in the decisions to produce and buy domestic goods (goods that are not traded internationally) and international goods. Under these assumptions we can develop a very simple geometric interpretation of the forces determining the equilibrium of the system.

In Figure 9-1 the price of domestic goods is plotted on the ordinate, and the price of international goods is plotted on the abscissa; because world prices are given, the exchange rate is equivalent to the price of international goods. On the assumption that international goods, domestic goods, and money are substitutes for one another in domestic consumption, the equilibrium lines specifying the locus of prices at which equilibrium will prevail in each of three markets will be as indicated.

The *II* schedule portraying the equilibrium line along which the demand for international goods is equal to the supply of international goods has a positive slope and is inelastic with respect to the *abscissa*, whereas the *DD* line which portrays the locus of prices along which the demand for domestic goods is equal to the supply of domestic goods has a positive slope but is inelastic with respect to the *ordinate*. The *MM* curve portrays the pattern of prices along which the community is willing to hold the existing stock of money, and tentatively is assumed to be fixed. Because there are only three objects of purchase in the system the three schedules intersect at a common point, *Q*, reflecting the interdependence of the three markets required by Walras' Law. In an equilibrium the price of goods and the exchange rate would be given respectively by the ordinate and abscissa indicated by the point *Q*. Points other than *Q* represent various situations of disequilibrium. We shall refer to a point in πe space as the "indicator."

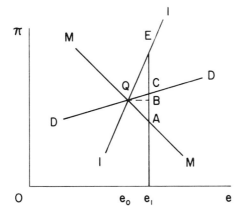

Figure 9-1

DEVALUATION

We are now ready to consider the effect of devaluation. Devaluation is an increase in the price of foreign exchange; because of our assumption that the terms of trade are constant, it implies an increase in the price of all international goods. Suppose the new exchange rate is Oe_1 so that the proportional devaluation is e_0e_1/Oe_0. The devaluation creates a disequilibrium, indicated by the point B, before any domestic prices have altered. At B there is an excess demand for domestic goods, an excess supply of international goods, and an excess demand for money. Because there is an excess demand for money, aggregate expenditure will be less than income as the community attempts to rebuild the real value of the cash balances destroyed by the devaluation. However, even though aggregate expenditure declines there can be, and in the diagram there must be, an excess demand for domestic goods; substitution effects in this case outweigh the liquidity effect of the devaluation.[2] There would thus be a tendency for domestic goods to rise in price, and the indicator might settle temporarily at the point C.

Can the indicator be held at the point C, a point of permanent equilibrium? At this point there is no excess demand for domestic goods, but there is an excess demand for money which implies both an excess of income over domestic expenditure and an equivalent excess supply of international goods. The excess supply of international goods is equivalent to a balance of payments surplus; in the absence of domestic credit creation by the banking system it implies an increase in exchange reserves, and in the absence of any reduction in the domestic assets of the banking system, the money supply. At the point C, therefore, the balance of payments surplus ensures an increase in the supply of money, while the excess of income over expenditure ensures an equivalent increase in the demand for money. The point C can therefore be a point of temporary monetary equilibrium.

It is only a temporary monetary equilibrium because portfolios are not in balance. The stock of money in the economy as a whole, in the absence of any sterilization operations, will be increasing; and an increase in the stock of money will alter the equilibrium configuration of the three schedules. The point Q will therefore gradually shift as the stock of money accumulates.

PORTFOLIO BALANCE

The extent to which the point Q shifts and the position of the new equilibrium are, in the real world, complicated by redistribution effects

2. DD would have a negative slope if domestic goods are complementary to international goods, as they may be in the case of a country producing raw materials; in this case the impact effect of devaluation can be deflationary.

and other dynamical side effects of devaluation. At the present level of abstraction, however, it is convenient to ignore all complications except those directly relevant to the meaning of devaluation itself. For simplicity, therefore, we can suppose that the new equilibrium lies along a ray OQ extended, at the point Q', in Figure 9-2. Suppose, for example, that the quantity of money increases in the same proportion as the price of foreign exchange. Then, assuming that the three real excess demand functions are homogeneous of zero-th degree in the three variables, π, e, and M, an equiproportionate increase in the quantity of money, devaluation, and an increase in the price of domestic goods would leave real excess demands unchanged. This establishes the justification for the point Q' as the new equilibrium.

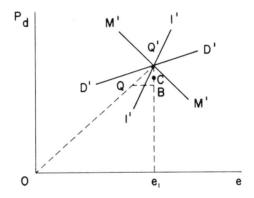

Figure 9-2   Devaluation Combined with an Equi-proportionate Expansion of Money

We can now construct three interpretations of the devaluation. The impact effect of the devaluation moves the indicator to the point B and subsequently to the point C after the domestic goods market has been equilibrated by a rise in the price of domestic goods, but before any changes in the supply of money have occurred; the point C lies on the original DD line. The point C, however, cannot remain the equilibrium because the balance of payments surplus at C will have monetary effects that will alter the position of the initial equilibrium, Q. To maintain the new exchange rate the central bank will be buying reserves and creating new domestic money. An increase in the money supply moves the point Q in the direction of point Q'.

There is, of course, more than one way in which the money supply can be increased: the central bank can buy domestic assets or it can buy foreign assets. A third possibility is that the central bank can increase the potential supply of currency at the time of devaluation in proportion to the rate of devaluation by creating a government deposit as a balancing item. In these three cases the money supply could increase more or less in proportion to the devaluation; but the final asset position of the central bank will differ in each case. Devaluation from a position of equilibrium *with no purchases of domestic assets* will cause an inflow of reserves that can only end when the real value of the original money supply is restored; if the original reserve ratio of the central bank equalled σ, reserves would increase by the multiple $\epsilon\,\sigma$, where ϵ is the rate of devaluation. For example, if foreign exchange or gold represented one-quarter of the banking system's assets, a devaluation of 10 percent would increase reserves by 40 percent.

As fundamental as this point is, it has been overlooked in the theoretical literature and in day-to-day policy of central banks. It is true that the central banks in Europe and in Japan have relied to a large extent on an increase in foreign exchange reserves as a means of generating an increase in domestic liquidity, whereas authorities like the Bank of England, through their exchange equalization account (created for use in 1932 when Britain had a flexible exchange system), up to 1968 tended to sterilize automatically the monetary effects of the balance of payments. For this reason we should expect devaluation by continental central banks to generate a substantial increase in reserves, while devaluation by a country that automatically neutralized the effect of foreign exchange purchases by increasing its domestic assets would not create the same gain in reserves. Even though the model here is highly simplified, it captures this important feature of real world experience relevant to countries that have engaged in devaluation. Unsuccessful devaluations should result from excessive extensions of domestic credit accompanying them.

DEVALUATION AND THE LEVEL OF RESERVES

In order to explore the theory of the relation between credit policy and the exchange rate in detail, it is necessary to study the structure of the banking system's assets. It is not directly relevant to our analysis whether we deal with the consolidated accounts of the entire banking system, or whether we confine our attention to the assets of the central bank. For simplicity, therefore, let us assume that there is only one bank, the central bank, in the economy.

The assets of the bank equal its liabilities. The liabilities can be divided into two parts: monetary liabilities, M, which we shall call the money supply; and nonmonetary liabilities, W, which we assume to be constant. It is also convenient to divide the bank's assets into two parts:

foreign assets or reserves, R', and other assets, Z. Since assets equal liabilities,

$$M + W = R' + Z. \tag{1}$$

This equation can also be written

$$R' + (Z - W) = M, \tag{2}$$

and because W is assumed constant we can simplify by defining $D = Z - W$, which we shall refer to as "domestic assets" in order to conform to the IMF concepts.

$$R' + D = M. \tag{3}$$

These terms are all measured in domestic currency.

For the purposes of devaluation analysis, however, reserves are usually defined in terms of foreign currency. Since e is the price of a unit of foreign exchange, we can write reserves in terms of foreign currency as

$$R = \frac{R'}{e} \tag{4}$$

so that instead of (3) we have

$$eR + D = M. \tag{5}$$

It is easy to see, from this formulation, how devaluation affects the assets and liabilities of the banking system. Devaluation is an increase in e. Differentiating the equation (5) and rearranging terms gives us

$$e\,\frac{dR}{de} = \frac{dM}{de} - \frac{dD}{de} - R = (\epsilon - \sigma)\frac{M}{e} - \frac{dD}{de}, \tag{6}$$

where $\epsilon = -(e/M)(dM/de)$ is the elasticity of the money supply with respect to the exchange rate and $\sigma = eR/M$ is the fraction of foreign reserves (reserve ratio) expressed in domestic currency, to the money supply.

It may facilitate understanding of this formula to suppose for a moment that the banking system does not change holdings of domestic assets (no open market operations or credit expansion) so that $dD/de = 0$. Then

$$\frac{dR}{de} = (\epsilon - \sigma)M. \tag{7}$$

This means that reserves increase or decrease depending on whether $\epsilon \gtrless \sigma$, that is, whether the percentage change in the money supply after devaluation is greater or less than the reserve ratio. Consider first the case where the central bank has no reserves so that $\sigma = 0$. Then reserves increase to the full extent of any increase in the money supply. This is because the only source of additional money creation is through asset purchases by the central bank; with no purchases of domestic assets, the entire basis of monetary expansion is the acquisition of foreign exchange.

Now consider the case where σ is not zero. Suppose, for illustrative purposes, that σ is equal to one-half, which means that reserves represent "backing" for one-half of the money supply. If the money supply increases in the same proportion as the devaluation ($\epsilon = 1$), then reserves must increase by an amount equal to half the money supply. The only source of money creation is additional purchases of foreign exchange, and given our assumption that there is no increase in domestic assets, this has to be generated by acquisition of reserves through the balance of payments.

Ordinarily some credit expansion will accompany devaluation. There are two reasons for this. The first is mechanical: the devaluation itself involves "profits." The domestic currency value of central bank assets rises after devaluation, and the "profits" will be credited to the government; this credit item of the government can be regarded as a monetary or a nonmonetary liability depending on whether government deposits are included as a component of the money supply. In the former case it becomes built into the ϵ; in the latter case it must be interpreted as an additional domestic asset.

Whether government deposits should be included or excluded from the money supply is a question of usefulness and will differ from country to country and government to government. If the government views aggregate monetary policy as one among many instruments of control it can shift deposits from the commercial bank to the central bank and back again, using that technique as one of the instruments of monetary policy. But if, as in many of the smaller countries, the government regards its additional cash deposits arising from the devaluation as a source of revenue to finance additional spending, government deposits can be incorporated into the definition of the money supply.

There is a second reason why credit expansion usually accompanies devaluation. The devaluation raises prices and thus reduces the real value of the money supply, making money "tight." To ease the adjustment process securities are sold, and unless capital is highly mobile internationally this will raise interest rates. To relieve the pressure on interest rates the authorities will generally expand credit, creating a monetary expansion over and above that which arises from the inflow of reserves. After devaluation the money supply is below its equilibrium level, and the community will adjust its expenditures in order to earn back the ordinary holdings of money needed for transactions and other purposes. But the required real adjustment in expenditure may be too rapid for the community to accept all at once, and the excessive borrowing that would result may cause too sudden an adjustment in interest rates and thus almost force some domestic credit expansion by the central bank. It should be realized that the credit operations will be at the expense of reserves.

WHEN DEVALUATION IS APPROPRIATE

Devaluation lowers the real value of government debt (both interest-yielding bonds and non-interest-yielding money), which is an asset of the public not entirely offset, from a psychological standpoint, by the capitalized value of future taxes. Devaluation, like a capital levy, is a tax. Current economic theory has tried to make it seem more respectable through emphasis on money illusion and its ability to cure unemployment. The pendulum of intellectual fashion has probably swung too far in that direction because short-run gains are achieved at a long-run cost. Leaving that issue aside, however, many countries have used the exchange rate as an instrument for maintaining independence of monetary policy. Devaluation or appreciation may be forced upon a country if prices have gotten out of line or if monetary adjustments become impossible.

The balance of payments, of course, is a monetary phenomenon, and its correction requires monetary policies. There are two methods of bringing about equilibrium. One is to change the *quantity* of money, the flexible money or fixed exchange rate solution; the other is to change the price of money, the fixed money or flexible exchange rate solution. If for some reason a country cannot follow a flexible monetary policy and has to give up the advantages of adhering to an international standard, it will occasionally have to resort to devaluation. This possibility naturally raises the question, when is devaluation appropriate?

In order to discover the cases under which devaluation is appropriate or necessary we need to examine the nature of the disequilibrium and try to infer from that the relation of the actual exchange rate and the actual level of liquidity in the economy to the equilibrium level of liquidity and the equilibrium exchange rate. For this purpose we can use Figure 9-3.

In Figure 9-3 we have changed the vertical axis from the price of domestic goods to the quantity of money. This enables us to treat the quantity of money in the system as a variable along with the exchange rate and to treat the price of domestic goods as a target to be achieved. The three schedules are, therefore, drawn up on the assumption that the price of domestic goods, as well as the wage rate, is constant.

The six zones in Figure 9-3 each reflect a given state of disequilibrium with respect to the three markets. Inflation or deflation applies when there is an excess demand or supply of domestic goods; deficit or surplus, when there is an excess demand or supply of international goods; and liquid or illiquid when there is excess supply or demand for money or, in terms of flows of resources, an excess of expenditure over income or income over expenditure.

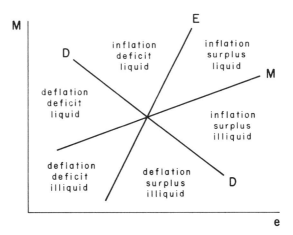

Figure 9-3

For every disequilibrium there is a corresponding appropriate rule of adjustment. If we know the nature of the disequilibrium we can discern whether a currency is over-valued or under-valued, or whether the money supply is in excess, of equilibrium, or is less than the equilibrium quantity. For example, Britain, in 1964, suffered from inflationary pressure, balance of payments deficit, and an excessively liquid economy; the appropriate step for Britain to follow to correct the disequilibrium was to deflate the excess liquidity from the economy—that is to say, to reduce the rate of credit expansion. Instead, the British imposed surtaxes and export subsidies with side effects that aggravated the basic disequilibrium. When the surtaxes were removed, the currency became overvalued and unemployment increased. Thus, by the summer of 1967 the British economy had moved into a position of deflation, balance of payments deficit, and excess liquidity, and the stage was set for devaluation. Subsequent to the devaluation the British economy required an increase in money, which was initially provided through internal credit expansion when it should have been provided through external monetization. It was only when credit ceilings were imposed that the deficit was turned into a surplus.

DEVALUATION AND THE TERMS OF TRADE IN A TWO-COUNTRY SETTING

The standard analysis of the effects of devaluation on the balance of payments can be greatly simplified and generalized by the methods developed here. However, it should be recognized at the outset that the

Bickerdike-Robinson-Metzler formula for the effect of devaluation on the balance of payments is subject to serious qualifications both with respect to relevance and interpretation. Let us first examine that approach, bearing in mind that the terms of trade are now allowed to change.

Let us conceive of an export good, x, and an import good, m; the balance of payments of the home country is

$$B = P_x x - P_m m, \tag{1}$$

where P_x is the local currency price of exports and P_m is the local currency price of imports. Differentiation yields

$$\frac{dB}{de} = x \frac{dP_x}{de} + P_x \frac{dx}{de} - P_m \frac{dm}{de} - em \frac{dP_m}{de}, \tag{2}$$

where e is the price of foreign exchange.

Now the demand and supply of both exports and imports can be taken as functions of the prices such that

$$x^d = x^d(P_x e, P_m e), \tag{3}$$

$$x^s = x^s(P_x, P_m), \tag{4}$$

$$m^d = m^d(P_m, P_x), \tag{5}$$

$$m^s = m^s(e P_m, e P_x), \tag{6}$$

where the superscripts denote demand or supply. By differentiation and formation of elasticities these functions can be expressed in terms of rates of change. Let η denote demand elasticities and Σ, supply elasticities. Then

$$\bar{x}^d = \eta_{xx}(\bar{P}_x + \bar{e}) + \eta_{xm}(\bar{P}_m + \bar{e}), \tag{7}$$

$$\bar{x}^s = \Sigma_{xx}\bar{P}_x + \Sigma_{xm}\bar{P}_m, \tag{8}$$

$$\bar{m}^d = \eta_{mm}\bar{P}_m + \eta_{mx}\bar{P}_x, \tag{9}$$

$$\bar{m}^s = \Sigma_{mm}(\bar{e} + \bar{P}_m) + \Sigma_{mx}(\bar{e} + \bar{P}_x), \tag{10}$$

where the bars over the variables indicate proportionate changes in the variables. Let us rewrite equation (2) as

$$\frac{dB}{P_x x} \equiv \bar{B} = \bar{x} + \bar{P}_x - T(\bar{m} + \bar{P}_m), \tag{11}$$

where

$$T \equiv \frac{P_m M}{P_x X}$$

Using (8) and (9) to eliminate $\bar{x}$ and $\bar{m}$ in (11), we get

$$\bar{B} = \Sigma_{xx}\bar{P}_x + \Sigma_{xm}\bar{P}_m + \bar{P}_x - T(\eta_{mm}\bar{P}_m + \eta_{mx}\bar{P}_x + \bar{P}_m)$$

or, in other words,

$$\bar{B} = (\Sigma_{xx} + 1 - T\eta_{mx})\bar{P}_x + (\Sigma_{xm} - T\eta_{mm} - T)\bar{P}_m. \qquad (12)$$

Setting $\bar{x}^d = \bar{x}^s$ in (7) and (8), and $\bar{m}^d = \bar{m}^s$ in (9) and (10) gives

$$(\eta_{xx} - \Sigma_{xx})\bar{P}_x + (\eta_{xm} - \Sigma_{xm})\bar{P}_m = -(\eta_{xx} + \eta_{xm})\bar{e} \qquad (13)$$

and

$$(\eta_{mx} - \Sigma_{mx})\bar{P}_x + (\eta_{mm} - \Sigma_{mm})\bar{P}_m = (\Sigma_{mm} + \Sigma_{mx})\bar{e}. \qquad (14)$$

Equations (12), (13), and (14) give us four variables, B, e, P_x, and P_m in three equations so that, given e or B, the other results can be established.

Let us first solve for the prices as functions of the exchange rate, using equations (13) and (14). We get

$$\frac{\bar{P}_x}{\bar{e}} = \frac{\begin{vmatrix} -\eta_{xx} - \eta_{xm} & \eta_{xm} - \Sigma_{xm} \\ \Sigma_{mm} + \Sigma_{mx} & \eta_{mm} - \Sigma_{mm} \end{vmatrix}}{\Delta} \qquad (15)$$

and

$$\frac{\bar{P}_m}{\bar{e}} = \frac{\begin{vmatrix} \eta_{xx} - \Sigma_{xx} & -\eta_{xx} - \eta_{xm} \\ \eta_{mx} - \Sigma_{mx} & \Sigma_{mm} + \Sigma_{mx} \end{vmatrix}}{\Delta}, \qquad (16)$$

where

$$\Delta = \begin{vmatrix} \eta_{xx} - \Sigma_{xx} & \eta_{xm} - \Sigma_{xm} \\ \eta_{mx} - \Sigma_{mx} & \eta_{mm} - \Sigma_{mm} \end{vmatrix}.$$

Thus, the change in the terms of trade is

$$\frac{\bar{P}_m - \bar{P}_x}{\bar{e}} = \frac{\begin{vmatrix} \eta_{xx} + \eta_{xm} & \Sigma_{xx} + \Sigma_{xm} \\ \Sigma_{mm} + \Sigma_{xx} & \eta_{mm} + \eta_{mx} \end{vmatrix}}{\Delta}. \qquad (17)$$

The conventional formulation is the special case of this result that obtains when we set

$$\eta_{xm} = \Sigma_{mx} = \Sigma_{xm} = \eta_{mx} = 0,$$

whence

$$\frac{\bar{P}_m - \bar{P}_x}{\bar{e}} = \frac{\begin{vmatrix} \eta_{xx} & \Sigma_{xx} \\ \Sigma_{mm} & \eta_{mm} \end{vmatrix}}{\Delta'},$$

where

$$\Delta' = (\eta_{xx} - \Sigma_{xx})(\eta_{mm} - \Sigma_{mm}),$$

the familiar criterion. But this result ignores the cross effects of price changes. It implies independence of P_x and P_m from one another, which could be an analytical relic of partial equilibrium reasoning or result from a fortuitous cancelling of opposite effects.

The reader is invited to solve for the effects of a change in the exchange rate on the balance of payments by substituting, say, equations (15) and (16) into equation (12) and seeing the traditional Bickerdike-Robinson-Metzler result emerge as a special case when the cross effects are set equal to zero. He should be warned, however, of the almost sterile nature of the exercise in a world in which money illusion is absent.

Considering the relation between the exchange rate and the balance of payments, note that it is unnecessary to go through all the algebra implied in solving for $\bar{B}/\bar{e}$ from equations (12), (13), and (14). This is because we know, from Walras' Law, that if the global markets for both import and export goods are cleared, the global demand for the two kinds of money must also be zero in the absence of domestic goods. In a no-credit economy, therefore, any excess demand for the money of one country has to equal the excess supply of money in the other country. The effect of a change in the exchange rate on the balance of payments thus reduces to its effect on the excess demand for one or the other currencies. By examining the effect of devaluation on the demand for money we can arrive at the effect on the balance of payments. The rate at which residents recover equilibrium cash balances determines, in the absence of central bank extensions of credit, the balance of payments.

The present procedure, however, suffers from the defect intrinsic in most analyses of the balance of payments, namely, a failure to ask the relevant question and to establish the correct time period of the analysis. The arbitrariness of assuming that the markets for traded goods are instantly cleared where other markets are not should be evident; at the limit it introduces the possibility of a separate theory of the balance of payments for each commodity in existence, depending on which markets are assumed to adjust quickly and which are delayed.[3]

3. For a discussion of the many country case in the context of the Hicks conditions, see my *International Economics* (New York: Macmillan Co., 1968), chap. 21.

chapter 10

interacting monetary areas

We shall now introduce a technique for analyzing the process of adjust-ment between two or more interacting monetary areas. Our method is to show first how two parts of the world, called countries, would establish an equilibrium if they were isolated from one another and then discuss the consequences of the opening up of exchange between them. For simplicity, I shall assume at the beginning that each country produces three com-modities X, Y, and G (gold), and that gold is used in each country as money; but later in the chapter we consider alternative currency arrange-ments.

AUTARKIC EQUILIBRIUM

Initially the two areas, designated by A and B, are assumed to be isolated from one another, and both establish autarkic equilibrium. These equilibria are established on the basis of the three interdependent equations for each country of the form

$$X^i = X^i(P^i_x, P^i_y, P^i_g) = 0,$$

$$Y^i = Y^i(P^i_x, P^i_y, P^i_g) = 0,$$

$$G^i = G^i(P^i_x, P^i_y, P^i_g) = 0,$$

where $i = a, b$ and the Ps are prices expressed in terms of an abstract unit of account. The three equations are restrained by the interdependence imposed by Walras' Law:

$$P_x^i X^i + P_y^i Y^i + P_g^i G^i = 0$$

so that any two of the equations suffice to establish equilibrium; because of Walras' Law, one of the equations could be dropped. Also, because of the homogeneity postulate which implies that only relative price changes affect excess demands, one of the variables can be eliminated. Division of P_x and P_y by P_g gives us an interdependent system involving equations for each country:

$$X^i(p_x^i, p_y^i) = 0,$$
$$Y^i(p_x^i, p_y^i) = 0,$$
$$G^i(p_x^i, p_y^i) = 0,$$

where $i = a, b$ and the ps now refer to gold prices. The interdependence of the three equations (Walras' Law) protects the system against inconsistency.

Gold prices of the two goods are represented on the abscissa and ordinate of Figure 10-1. The autarkic equilibria are designated by the points Qa and Qb in Figure 10-1 where the points are determined by the solution of the equation system. The XX, YY, and GG schedules applicable for each country portray the conditions of equilibrium in the markets for

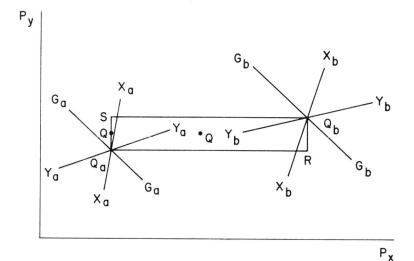

Figure 10-1

X, Y, and G, respectively, and are drawn on the assumption that the goods are substitutes in each country. This assumption implies that the XX and YY schedules are inelastic with respect to the abscissa and ordinate, respectively, and that the GG curves have negative slopes.

EXCHANGE EQUILIBRIUM

The opening up of the possibility of exchange implies that price ratios can differ by no more than the margins permitted by the artificial and real impediments to exchange. We ignore these impediments so that exchange equilibrium implies equality of prices. The equations of equilibrium are now

$$X^a + X^b = 0,$$

$$Y^a + Y^b = 0,$$

$$G^a + G^b = 0,$$

which means that we have dropped three equations, two of which were "effective." However, we get them back by the equations specifying the elimination of arbitrage profits:

$$P^a_x = P^b_x, \quad P^a_y = P^b_y.$$

Thus we drop two equations and two unknowns.

Where will the trade equilibrium be? First, let us treat gold as if it were an ordinary traded commodity like X and Y in order to determine a short-run flow equilibrium. As the diagram is drawn we have, before trade, $P^a_x < P^b_x$ and $P^a_y < P^b_y$. Thus gold is initially cheaper in terms of both X and Y in country B, so it will flow from B to A in exchange for X and Y, lowering P^b_x and P^b_y and raising P^a_x and P^a_y. The new equilibrium, therefore, will be enclosed within the rectangle $Q_a R Q_b S$.

Analytically, we can find this new equilibrium by aggregating the excess demand schedules into world excess demand schedules; or, what amounts to the same thing, by finding the point at which the excess demand for each good in one country is balanced by an equivalent excess supply in the other country. This common point is designated in Figure 10-1 by the point Q, which represents trade equilibrium. X will be exported from A to B, G will be exported from B to A, and Y will be exported from A to B or B to A depending on whether $Y_a Y_a$ is above (to the left of) or below (to the right of) $Y_b Y_b$.

GOLD AND PORTFOLIO BALANCE

The preceding analysis shows how the opening up of trade results in the establishment of equilibrium world prices, but it does not make a sufficient distinction between gold as an indestructible monetary resource and the flow of nongold commodities which are exchanged and consumed in ordinary consumption. The point Q can be interpreted as a temporary equilibrium established at the outset of trade, but this equilibrium cannot last indefinitely. If gold is desired solely for its use as money it will generate changes in stocks which will end only when gold holdings as an asset in the community's wealth portfolios are in balance. Apart from the use of gold as an ordinary commodity and abstracting from secular growth, which can lead to a steady increase in the desired stock of gold, a longer-run equilibrium will eventually be established when trade in gold ceases. Let us, therefore, look upon gold only as money, fixed in amount for the world as a whole, and assume there is no growth. To analyze the problem we need to develop the mathematical model in a slightly different way, by treating gold as a stock.

We can introduce gold stocks directly into the excess demand equations and thus write the world excess demand equations for the two goods as follows:

$$X^a(P_x, P_y, G^a) + X^b(P_x, P_y, G^b) = 0,$$

$$Y^a(P_x, P_y, G^a) + Y^b(P_x, P_y, G^b) = 0.$$

These equations must now be supplemented by the balance of payments identities:

$$P_x X^a + P_y Y^a + h_a = \frac{dG^a}{dt},$$

and

$$(P_x X^b + P_y Y^b) + h_n = \frac{dG^b}{dt},$$

where h_a and h_b denote desired hoarding in the two countries. We also have

$$G^a + G^b = \overline{G}$$

where $\overline{G}$ is the world gold stock, so that

$$\frac{dG^a}{dt} + \frac{dG^b}{dt} = 0.$$

It is clear that, as long as gold stocks are shifting locations, excess demands and prices will be changing so that the system can only settle down in equilibrium when gold flows have ceased.

We now regard the country excess demand functions as homogeneous of degree zero in P_x, P_y, and G^i, and this enables us to show geometrically the nature of the equilibrium that will establish itself. This is done in Figure 10-2, which duplicates some of the features of Figure 10-1.

When gold flows from B to A, as it does upon the opening up of trade, it increases A's gold stock, shifting the point Q_a outward along the ray OQ_a; and it decreases B's gold stock, shifting the point Q_b inward along the ray OQ_b. This process stops only when trade in gold has ceased, that is, when the balance of payments of the two countries has been brought into equilibrium. This will occur when the excess demand for gold in *each* country is zero. In other words, the final equilibrium will be at a point like Q, which need not correspond to Q in Figure 10-1, where the gold equilibrium lines in each country, $G_a'G_a'$ and $G_b'G_b'$, coincide at one point at least.

At the equilibrium Q there is no trade in money, and the value of A's exports of X and B's exports of Y are equal to one another. Gold stocks become redistributed between the two countries along the lines of Ricardo's "theorem" on the uniqueness of the distribution of the precious metals. The terms of trade settle in between the pretrade ratios, and in the diagram are given by the slope of OQ.

INCONVERTIBLE CURRENCIES AND
FLEXIBLE EXCHANGE RATES

It is a short step from this point to adapt the apparatus to represent a system in which there are separate national currencies. This requires a redefinition of prices. Let the prices of X and Y in the two countries be expressed in terms of local currencies, and assume as before that pretrade equilibrium is at Q_a and Q_b as in Figure 10-3. Assume also that the residents of each country hold only national currency, no "Euro-dollars," and that exchange rates are flexible.

Under these conditions there is no meaning to the statement that prices will be the "same" in the two countries, since prices are expressed in different things. What must be equalized, however, are the *relative* prices of X and Y; there will be common terms of trade. To find the equilibrium terms of trade, rotate the ray OQ between the autarkic rays OQ_a and OQ_b until the excess supply of X in A (the value of the excess demand for Y in A along A's money equilibrium line) equals the excess

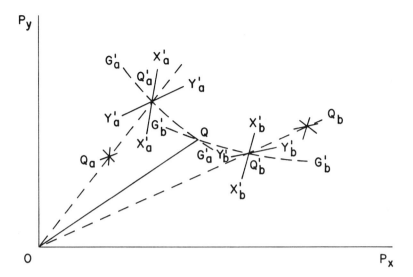

Figure 10-2

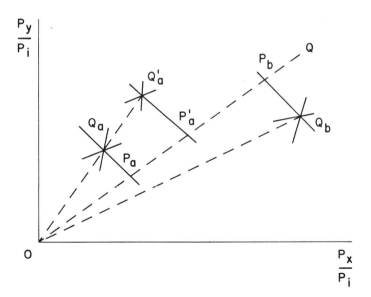

Figure 10-3

demand for X in B (the value of the excess supply of Y in B along B's money equilibrium line). There will be at least[1] one such ray, and this will establish points P_a and P_b at which trade will be balanced. The exchange rate between the two currencies is given by the ratio OP_a/OP_b.

PURCHASING POWER PARITY

The same diagram (Figure 10-3) can also be used to illustrate Cassel's purchasing power parity doctrine. Suppose the money supply in country A is increased in the proportion OQ'_a/OQ_a. Then, abstracting from hysteresis effects connected with the adjustment process, redistribution effects associated with debtor-creditor wealth positions, transactions costs arising from the costs of menu changing, and money illusion, the new autarkic point would be at Q'_a. This implies that A's prices will rise to P'_a and the exchange rate will depreciate in the proportion $P_aP'_a/OP$, giving a new price of B's currency in terms of A's currency equal to OP'_a/OP_b. A given percentage change in one country's money supply will cause an equi-proportionate increase in all prices, including the price of B's currency. The purchasing power parity doctrine is a straightforward extension of the homogeneity postulate and the quantity theory of money.

The methods used here are readily adapted to the transfer problem and a specific consideration of interest rates. It suffices to specify that the prices are for present and future goods and that the slope of the indicator to the origin is unity plus or minus the rate of interest.

---

1. The theoretical possibility of unstable equilibria means that there may be more than one such ray in the actual world, although this possibility is ruled out by our assumption that the goods are substitutes.

chapter 11   multilateral policy and exchange rate changes

The problem under analysis in this part is a real world problem that existed in 1968; here, however, we shall abstract from the political and many of the economic variables that have to be associated with contributions to policy. Our purpose is to use the problem to show how the general equilibrium approach to exchange rates can illuminate the subject and add to our stock of theoretical knowledge.

THE EXCHANGE MARKET DISEQUILIBRIUM

The disequilibrium in the exchange markets has been apparent for some months now,[1] although opinions differ on the question of whether the disequilibrium is transitory and easily correctable, or fundamental and intractable without a basic realignment of exchange parities. Casual observation suggests the following:

1. The deutsche mark is "undervalued" with respect to the dollar.
2. The French franc is "overvalued" with respect to the dollar.
3. All currencies are "overvalued" with respect to gold.

1. This was written in October 1968. The French franc was devalued in August 1969, and the German mark was revalued two months later.

Appearances can be deceiving, however, because current balances on the markets are connected with stocks of assets and speculation; we will take the appearances for reality in this chapter in order to focus on theoretical rather than practical issues.

The terms under- and overvaluation have to be used circumspectly. They suggest specific actions: namely, adjustment of the *DM* and *FF* exchange rates and a uniform reduction in the value of all currencies against gold. But this is only one approach to adjustment. An alternative approach could involve credit expansion in Germany, contraction in France, and worldwide contraction to make the current gold price one of equilibrium. Another set of alternatives would involve a combination of internal and external adjustments. For example, Germany might expand credit, France might devalue against the dollar, and all currencies could change vis-a-vis gold.

There are additional possibilities. The disequilibrium could be corrected by the introduction of substitutes. It is possible, for example, that the creation of a new international money could so reduce the demand for gold that a change in par values is not necessary. Gold could be partially or completely replaced as an international reserve asset by a substitute.

Our purpose in this chapter, however, is not to recommend but to analyze. What light does general equilibrium theory shed on the currency problem? To simplify the argument I shall assume that changes in the exchange rates are the only instruments available.

FRENCH DEFICITS AND GERMAN SURPLUSES

Suppose we start from a position of general equilibrium and imagine that this equilibrium is disturbed by exogenous changes. Suppose, in particular, that productivity increases in Germany, unaccompanied by corresponding increases in monetary expenditure, lead to a situation where the deutsche mark is undervalued relative to other currencies. Further, suppose that a temporary disorganization of production in France, unaccompanied by corresponding reductions in money income, creates a situation in which the deutsche mark is undervalued while the French franc is overvalued. The upshot of these occurrences may be a position similar to that illustrated in Figure 11-1.

The line *MM* depicts the pattern of exchange rates that would permit equilibrium in Germany; *FF* provides an analogous curve for France. Initial equilibrium is supposed to be at the point *P*, but disturbances generate changes leading to a new equilibrium at *Q*.

The policymaker acts without complete information. He knows the

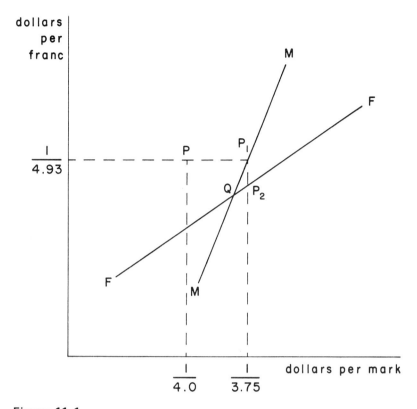

Figure 11-1

existing exchange rates, and he observes the disequilibrium in the exchange market. Under fixed exchange rates the Bundesbank will be buying dollars and supplying marks, and the Bank of France will be selling dollars and buying francs. Either or both countries may be partially or completely neutralizing the monetary flows by corresponding credit advances in France and credit restrictions in Germany.

The problem of adjustment is the problem of reestablishing equilibrium. Under fixed exchange rates this would involve policies which bring the *FF* and *MM* schedules back so that they intersect at the point *P*; in general, this will involve expenditure increases in Germany and expenditure decreases in France. The focus of our problem, however, is to preserve internal conditions in the countries and achieve balance through appropriate exchange rate changes.

The adjustment is more complicated than it appears on the diagram because we have not taken into account a number of complicating factors such as stocks and flows; we will ignore these complications here because our purpose is more general. What sequence of changes is likely to lead to equilibrium?

Suppose first that the German authorities widen the exchange margins, or, more simply, abandon central bank intervention in the market for marks. This would lead to a position at P_1 where the mark price of the dollar is, say, DM 3.75. German balance is restored, and the French balance is improved; but the French balance is not entirely eliminated, while the appreciation of the mark will have improved the balances of other countries in the system, throwing them out of equilibrium. Further adjustments are therefore required.

Suppose now the French franc is set free, and the mark rate kept at 3.75. The franc will depreciate and generate a new position at P_2, which will in turn shift part of the deficit back to Germany and thus create the need for a sequence of exchange rate changes, bringing about a convergent process ultimately leading to the equilibrium at Q.

The German authorities might be able to guess at the new equilibrium of the system. If they could be sure that France would devalue, they might let the mark float up to $1/3.75$ and then peg it at some lower amount, such as $1/3.8$, anticipating French devaluation. But it would be extremely unlikely that any discrete exchange rate changes would lead to an equilibrium relationship and thus obviate the need for internal adjustment.

My purpose now, however, is to illuminate a different aspect of the problem. The point Q represents an equilibrium for the franc and the mark. But will it also be an equilibrium for other currencies as well? That is the problem to which I now want to turn.

In a world in which there were only marks, francs, and dollars, the equilibrium would be a general one since the sum of the *excess* demands for marks, francs, and dollars would be identically zero, following Cournot's Law. This could be represented diagrammatically by drawing a line with a negative slope through P, showing the exchange rates at which the United States is in equilibrium. But under what conditions would this line, which I shall refer to as the DD curve, go through P in a world in which the third "good" of the system, represented by dollars, is not a homogeneous good?

From a theoretical point of view we can adopt the Leontief-Hicks theorem of composite commodities and lump all goods together, for analytical purposes, if their prices move together in the same proportion. But this proposition has to be interpreted carefully. It does not mean that we can assume zero excess demands for each of the remaining components in the composite commodity bundle. If the pound, other currencies, and gold are convertible into the dollar at exchange rates fixed by the central banks, we can treat constancy of relative prices as a special case of "moving in the same proportion," and draw up the *FF*, *MM*, and *DD* curves on this assumption. But the *DD* curve represents, not the equilibrium schedule for the United States dollar, but the equilibrium schedule for the composite commodity bundle of assets. If we are interested specifically in the balance of payments of countries within the composite commodity group, we cannot assume that the point *Q* represents an equilibrium for each country's balance. For each balance to be in equilibrium at *P*, it is required that each relative price within the bundle not only be constant, but be at its equilibrium level. For each target there has to correspond an instrument of equilibrium, and if we are interested in the overall balance, all the instruments have to be in line with one another. To say that at *Q* the French and German balances are in equilibrium implies that the *sum* of all remaining balances is zero, but not that each individual balance is zero. And when rates within the composite bundle are changed, *Q* will no longer, in general, reflect the equilibrium exchange rates of the mark and the franc.

In order to explore the problem arising from these multiple market considerations it will be convenient to make a distinction between different assets in the composite bundle. Suppose we divide up the composite bundle into gold and other things (dollars plus all currencies and goods convertible into dollars at a given price) which we call "dollars." We can then analyze a model including marks, francs, gold, and dollars, the *dollar* prices of which will be designated by p_m, p_f, p_g, and 1. We have then four excess demand equations to determine the three equilibrium prices:

$$X_m(p_m, p_f, p_g) = 0, \tag{1}$$

$$X_f(p_m, p_f, p_g) = 0, \tag{2}$$

$$X_g(p_m, p_f, p_g) = 0, \tag{3}$$

$$X_d(p_m, p_f, p_g) = 0, \tag{4}$$

rendered consistent by Cournot's Law:

$$p_m X_m + p_f X_f + p_g X_g + X_d = 0. \tag{5}$$

The last identity can be used to eliminate one of the redundant market equations. For example, the identity (5) can be written

$$X_g = -\left(\frac{p_m}{p_g}\right) X_m - \left(\frac{p_f}{p_g}\right) X_f - \left(\frac{1}{p_g}\right) X_d, \tag{6}$$

and if we substitute the functional forms for the excess demands from equations (1), (2), and (4), we already have equation (3). It makes no difference, apart from matters of presentation, which equation is omitted.[2]

Suppose now that we solve the system for the equilibrium price of gold, p_g^0. *Given* this equilibrium price, we can solve the reduced equation system

$$X_m(p_m, p_f; p_g^0) = 0, \tag{7}$$

$$X_f(p_m, p_f; p_g^0) = 0, \tag{8}$$

$$X_d(p_m, p_f; p_g^0) = 0, \tag{9}$$

to find the equilibrium exchange rate for the mark and the franc vis-a-vis the dollar, arriving at an equilibrium such as that portrayed by the point Q in Figure 11-1, and duplicated by the point Q in Figure 11-2.

UNDERVALUED GOLD

The thrust of our current emphasis, however, is the situation prevailing when the relative prices in the composite commodity bundle are *not* in equilibrium. Suppose the dollar price of gold is *not* at its equilibrium level. In particular, suppose the dollar price of gold is *below* its equilibrium level.

To investigate the theoretical implications of this possibility, we can start off with the equilibrium prices and differentiate the system with respect to the price of gold, treating it now as a parameter. What effect will this have on the position of the three curves that, before the change, simultaneously met at the point Q?

Equations (7), (8), and (9) are equilibrium conditions. We have to consider now disequilibrium conditions. To do so we shall leave unspecified, at the moment, whether each excess demand is zero.

2. The reader familiar with the controversies of monetary theory—in particular, the dispute in the 1940s between protagonists of the Robertsonian loanable funds theory and the Keynesian liquidity preference theory—should recognize the analogy. That controversy was due to imprecise concepts used in referring to the meaning of "determining" a particular price in a general equilibrium context. What does it mean to say that a price is "determined" in a market when many variables affect the excess demand functions? If the money equations are eliminated, we are left with a loanable funds theory of interest; if the bond equations are eliminated, we are left with a liquidity preference theory of interest. The ensuing exchanges gave rise to Lerner's famous quip that "if we eliminate the peanuts equations, we get a peanuts theory of interest."

The issue has presumably now been resolved to everyone's satisfaction; the original difficulty was in the identification of the term "determining" with dynamics. When one of the static equations was eliminated first, dynamical equations were then formulated in a manner that was symmetrical with the eliminated market equation. Patinkin contributed to an important clarification of this issue, and I have examined the mathematical issues in some detail, in the context of the choice of a "key currency" in my *International Economics* (New York: Macmillan Co., 1968), chap. 21, esp. pp. 310–13.

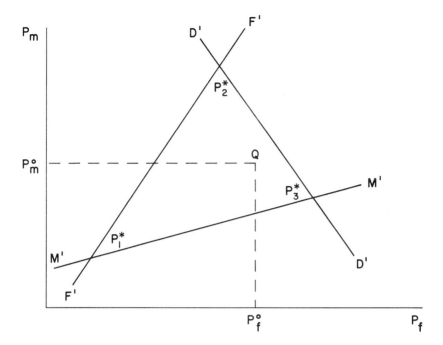

Figure 11-2

By differentiation of (7), (8), and (9) with respect to p_g, but leaving unspecified the value of each dX_i, we get

$$\frac{\partial X_m}{\partial p_m}\frac{dp_m}{dp_g} + \frac{\partial X_m}{\partial p_f}\frac{dp_f}{dp_g} = -\frac{\partial X_m}{\partial p_g} + \frac{dX_m}{dp_g},\tag{10}$$

$$\frac{\partial X_f}{\partial p_m}\frac{dp_m}{dp_g} + \frac{\partial X_f}{\partial p_f}\frac{dp_f}{dp_g} = -\frac{\partial X_f}{\partial p_g} + \frac{dX_f}{dp_g},\tag{11}$$

$$\frac{\partial X_d}{\partial p_m}\frac{dp_m}{dp_g} + \frac{\partial X_d}{\partial p_f}\frac{dp_f}{dp_g} = -\frac{\partial X_d}{\partial p_g} + \frac{dX_d}{dp_g}.\tag{12}$$

In order to determine the shifts in the curves that take place when the price of gold changes, we need to know the signs of the partial derivatives. I assume that all assets are gross substitutes. This means that an increase in the price of gold will, ceteris paribus, reduce the demand for gold and increase the demand for marks, francs, and dollars[3] so that each of the terms on the right of (10), (11), and (12) (exclusive of the minus sign) is positive. It means, further, that

3. I hope to explore the implications of this assumption in the context of international currency systems in depth at a later date.

$$\frac{\partial X_m}{\partial p_m} < 0; \frac{\partial X_m}{\partial p_f} > 0; \frac{\partial X_f}{\partial p_m} > 0; \frac{\partial X_f}{\partial p_f} < 0; \frac{\partial X_d}{\partial p_m} > 0; \frac{\partial X_d}{\partial p_f} > 0.$$

When we attempt to solve the three equations for the two price changes by setting each $dX_i = 0$, we can see at once that we are faced with a problem of overdeterminacy. This arises because the three equilibrium equations are independent of one another. We cannot make use of Walras' Law because we have already made use of it in eliminating the gold market equation. There is not one solution to these equations, but three solutions!

It is tempting at this point to throw up one's hands in despair and to suppose that we have committed an atrocious logical error in setting up the equations of the system. But this is not so. In fact, the three solutions implied by the mathematical system provide us with a necessary insight into the economics of the currency system and the requirements of balance of payments adjustment.

Let us proceed systematically. If we set $(dX_m/dp_g) = (dX_f/dp_g) = 0$, we then have three equations in the three unknowns, (dp_m/dp_g), (dp_f/dp_g) and (dX_d/dp_g). It is readily shown that $(dX_d/dp_g) > 0$, so that if gold is undervalued, as it is when the price of gold is lowered from its equilibrium value, flexible exchange rates or wider margins restoring balance of payments equilibrium in the exchange markets of Germany and France will leave the U.S. balance of payments in a deficit exactly corresponding to the excess demand for gold.

To determine the values of (dp_m/dp_g) and (dp_f/dp_g), we need to use an additional property of the system: the homogeneity postulate. If abstract prices of the franc, the mark, the dollar, *and* gold were raised in the same proportion, excess demands would be unchanged if the system were homogeneous of degree zero.[4] In that case, a decrease in the dollar price of gold, with the mark-dollar and the franc-dollar exchange rates free to adjust, would lead to the same qualitative changes in prices as an increase in the gold price of the dollar, with the mark-dollar and the franc-dollar exchange rates free to adjust. Given the gross substitutes assumption, this implies that the Hicks conditions of perfect stability are satisfied and that the equilibrium dollar prices of the marks and francs are higher.

We thus arrive at a new equilibrium in Figure 11-2 represented by the intersection of $M'M'$ and $F'F'$ at the point P_1^*. By similar reasoning we can show that the dollar line $D'D'$ shifts upward, forming new equilibria at P_2^*, where the franc price of gold and the dollar price of gold but not

4. Note that this is *not* the same as saying that if there were a uniform reduction in the IMF par values of all currencies excess demands would be unchanged, since par values are defined in terms of gold and that change would, therefore, involve a relative change in the price of gold in terms of all currencies, which would necessarily affect excess demands because it would alter the currency (and commodity) values of all gold holdings via the international real balance effect.

the mark price, are allowed to adjust; and at P_3^*, where the dollar and mark prices of gold adjust, but not the franc price of gold.

Let us go back then to consider the implications of a situation in which there is an excess supply of francs, an excess demand for marks, and gold is undervalued in terms of all currencies. This situation is portrayed in Figure 11-3 by the point P. It is obvious that there does not exist a set of exchange rate changes vis-a-vis the dollar that will restore equilibrium in all markets. An appreciation of the mark alone to establish the point P_1 would eliminate the German surplus; appreciation to the point P_2 would correct the U.S. deficit; or a devaluation of the franc combined with adjustment of the mark to reach the point P_3 would correct the German and French balances. But simultaneous equilibrium in all markets is not possible without a change in the value of the dollar relative to gold.

MUSICAL CHAIRS

The interesting question is what happens to the system when it is faced with the impossible task of trying to adjust to an equilibrium that does not exist.

One answer is that the system flits from one quasi equilibrium to another. Suppose there were a devaluation of the franc and perhaps an appreciation of the mark sufficient to restore "equilibrium" at P_3. At

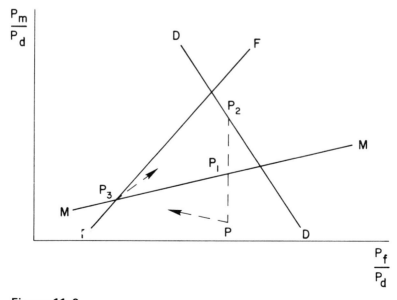

Figure 11-3

this point there is an excess supply of dollars and an excess demand for gold. This disequilibrium could be associated either with involuntary dollar accumulations on the part of the European countries and inflationary pressure in Europe (shifting the *FF* and *MM* curves to the right and upwards, respectively, and moving the point P_3 to the northeast); or it could mean conversions of dollars into gold at the U.S. Treasury, destroying international reserves and perhaps forcing deflationary pressure on the U.S. (bringing *DD* down to the left). In both of these cases of internal adjustment, there is an implosion of the system. When the "burden" is shared among all countries, the three curves draw inward toward each other until the three vortices of the disequilibrium triangle are brought together.

In the context of the model there are only two solutions: an increase in the price of gold, or general world deflation. The three points can be brought together only by a deflationary implosion of the system or by a restoration of the equilibrium relation between gold and the dollar through an increase in the price of gold in terms of all currencies. This is the logic of the case for an increase in the price of gold as a resolution of current world problems in the absence of new gold substitutes.

chapter 12

should the united states devalue the dollar?

THE LEGAL SYSTEM

What does devaluation of the dollar mean? There is some ambiguity in this question that confuses even the people who can be expected to understand the exchange system. It could have one of three meanings:

a. An increase in the official price of gold in terms of the dollar and all other currencies; technically this is a uniform *reduction* in the par value of all currencies.

b. A *reduction* in the par value of the dollar as established at the IMF, all other par values remaining constant.

c. An *increase* in the par value of all (or some) other currencies relative to the par value of the U.S. dollar.

It could also mean a rise in the price of commodities. We will eliminate that possibility since no one is advocating that kind of devaluation.

It is a rather amusing commentary on the division of knowledge within social sciences that lawyers tend to think that there is no economic difference between the three types of devaluation, while some economists think there is no legal difference. But it is important to keep both the legal and economic distinctions in mind.

Adapted from "Should the United States Devalue the Dollar?" *Western Economic Journal* 6 (Sept. 1968): 247–59.

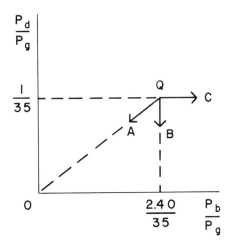

Figure 12-1

These three possibilities are illustrated in Figure 12-1. On the ordinate we place the price of dollars expressed in terms of gold, and on the abscissa the price of the pound sterling in terms of gold. We shall use the price of the pound sterling for the moment as representative of the price of all foreign currencies.[1] Each point in the graph indicates three price ratios: the gold price of the dollar, the gold price of sterling, and, implicitly, the dollar price of the pound (the reciprocal of the slope of a ray connecting the origin and the point, such as the line OQ).

Let us consider now "devaluation" of the dollar. This could mean a reduction in the price of the dollar in terms of gold, the gold price of the pound being constant: a movement in the direction B. It could mean an increase in the price of gold in terms of both the dollar and the pound: a movement in the direction A. Or it could mean a reduction in the price of the dollar in terms of the pound, the dollar price of gold remaining constant (an appreciation of the pound): a movement in the direction C. What considerations are involved in selecting one or the other?

First, we should clarify the legal system. The unit of account in the IMF system is gold, not dollars; par values are defined in gold or "1944 gold dollars." The term "gold dollars" sometimes gives rise to confusion. This results from the failure to distinguish between two meanings of a unit of account: a unit of *quotation* and a unit of *contract*. In domestic monetary systems these are invariably the same, but in the international monetary system the *dollar* is the unit of quotation while *gold* is the unit of contractual

---

1. This is legitimate because we are assuming implicitly that the prices of all foreign currencies are constant relative to each other, and we can therefore utilize the Hicks-Leontief theorem on the composition of "commodities."

obligations. This means that if the U.S. alone lowered the par value of the dollar, the dollar price of gold would be raised and, legally, so would the dollar price of all foreign currencies; we would move in the direction *B*. Thus, when we consider devaluation of the dollar in the same sense that we consider devaluation of any other currency, we mean an increase in the dollar price of gold *and* an increase in the dollar price of every other currency. This is because gold is the legal unit of contractual obligation in the IMF Agreement.

To change exchange rates it is not enough, however, for the U.S. to change the par value of the dollar. It is necessary also that the par values of some of the other members of the fund stay constant or be reduced by a smaller proportion. A change in exchange rates involves a change in the slope of the ray OQ, but the U.S., acting alone within the framework of the Articles, can only determine (in consultation with the IMF) its vertical position on the graph. Because other countries have control over horizontal positions, they can cancel any change in the slope the U.S. may wish to make. This is why exchange rate changes have to be made, or at least are most effectively made, in consultation with an international body.

To change the price of gold in terms of all currencies requires a majority of the weighted votes in the IMF, subject to veto by any member who has over 10 percent of the voting power.[2] A uniform reduction in par values is not, therefore, within the control of the U.S. alone, although the U.S. has a veto power over such a change.

The only independent option for the U.S. is to change its par value, although the exercise of this option does not imply that other countries would allow the devaluation to permit a change in exchange rates. Since the U.S. has not exercised its 10 percent option, it could still change its par value by 10 percent after notifying the fund and getting the approval of Congress.

Prior to the new amendments to the Articles of Agreement, the executive board could waive the maintenance-of-gold-value clause of fund assets with a simple majority vote. Now this decision will be reserved for the Board of Governors and requires an 85 percent majority; this change was instituted to give the E.E.C. a veto and it means, effectively, that a world-wide doubling of the price of gold would be associated with a doubling of the size of the fund, and that the fund provides an escape through which other countries can acquire a gold value guarantee on a portion of their foreign exchange reserves.

So much for legal complications. Legally, gold is the unit of contract. We can say that gold is the de jure numeraire. But the "economic numer-

---

2. The new amendments have altered this provision in order to withdraw the veto privilege from the U.K., and to give it to the European Economic Community; a uniform change in par values will require an 85 percent majority.

aire" is the dollar. The dollar is the *intervention currency*, the currency that is used in the exchange markets by foreign central banks to stabilize exchange rates of other member currencies against their own within a margin of 1 percent on either side of parity.[3] Formally this would mean that each country would have to concern itself with $n - 1$ exchange rates, where n is the number of members. The n countries collectively would be involved in $n (n - 1)$ price commitments altogether of which, of course, only $\frac{1}{2}$ of $n (n - 1)$ would be effective since either country can perform the stabilization function. If the division of labor on this were shared with each country protecting, say, its lower bound, there would be again $n (n - 1)$ "desks" needed to fix rates.

Obviously, multilateral intervention of this kind would lead to a very complicated system. A centralized pegging system is clearly more efficient. Thus, early in the fund's history, it was agreed that fixing rates in terms of the dollar within the margins would fulfill the legal requirements. This was the origin of the dollar's role as an intervention currency.

THE MARKET SYSTEM

In the market system, by contrast with the legal system, the emphasis is on the *dollar price of gold* and the *dollar price of other currencies* rather than the gold prices of currencies. The dollar is the numeraire, and it is more natural to transform the coordinates of the graph to reflect this fact. The same information is contained in Figure 12-2 as in Figure 12-1, and the vectors corresponding to *A*, *B*, and *C* in Figure 12-1 are *A'*, *B'*, and *C'* in Figure 12-2. All we have done is to change the frame of reference.

Now consider again the meaning of devaluation. Suppose the U.S. "devalues" in the legal sense, and we say that other countries do "nothing." Nothing here can mean nothing in the *jurisphere*, or nothing in the *ecosphere*. If exchange market operators stand pat so that exchange rates remain fixed to the dollar, all countries except the U.S. would be in violation of the fund's rules. If, on the other hand, countries continue to comply with fund rules, they have to appreciate their exchange rates with respect to the dollar. Ceteris paribus "juris" means something different from ceteris paribus "ecos!"

We have raised these various meanings of the term "devaluation" not because they are important in themselves, but primarily to show why it is that people get confused about the meaning of dollar devaluation. It is

3. Actually, somewhat wider margins are permitted to allow for the wider spreads that result when the major countries peg their rates to the dollar, while some other countries peg their exchange rates to the pound sterling, the French franc, or the Portuguese escudo; the fund regulations permit wider spreads (up to about two percent) as a "multiple-currency practice."

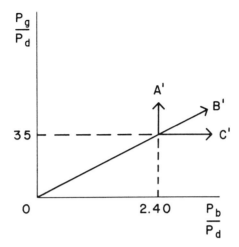

Figure 12-2

hard not to get confused about it. The difficulty arises from the role of gold as a unit of contract and measure, and the role of the dollar as the unit of quotation and intervention.

But enough of technicalities. Let us turn to the economics of the subject.

THE ECONOMICS OF DEVALUATION

Let us conceive of a world of three goods called dollars, gold, and pounds. Forget about their roles as money; for the moment they are just any three goods. Equilibrium prices are established by market balance equations. If P_d, P_g and P_b denote the abstract prices[4] of these three goods, expressed in terms of an abstract unit of account, we can write three excess demand equations,

$$X'_d (P_d, P_g, P_b) = 0 \tag{1}$$

$$X'_g (P_d, P_g, P_b) = 0 \tag{2}$$

$$X'_b (P_d, P_g, P_b) = 0 \tag{3}$$

to determine the three unknowns, P_d, P_g, and P_b.

We have, however, a problem with such a system. The system of real excess demands is homogeneous of degree zero in the three abstract prices. So we can "normalize" them by taking one good, say gold, as the numeraire. Then we get three equations in two relative prices:

4. An "abstract price" has a single dimension, Q^{-1}.

$$X'_d (P_d, p_b) = 0 \tag{4}$$

$$X'_g (P_d, p_b) = 0 \tag{5}$$

$$X'_b (P_d, p_b) = 0. \tag{6}$$

We would be in trouble now if the three equations were independent. But if the system is closed the markets are connected by Walras' Law:

$$p_d X_d + X_g + p_b X_b \equiv 0. \tag{7}$$

Thus, any two of the equations will give us equilibrium gold prices, and the other equation must be compatible with that equilibrium.

Let us assume that the three goods are substitutes. Then the system can be presented diagrammatically as in Figure 12-3. Each of the lines graphs one of the equations (B for pounds, D for dollars, G for gold), and the six zones reflect potential positions of disequilibrium. But the apparatus gives us a general equilibrium framework for analysis.

A country does not devalue unless it is in disequilibrium. Our concern is, ultimately, to find the circumstances of disequilibrium that justify devaluation. But to do so we need to know the effects of devaluation. So we start at the equilibrium Q and ask: what will be the consequences of devaluation?

We are thus back to the question posed in the beginning. What kind of devaluation are we talking about? Let us proceed systematically.

Devaluation in the sense (a) (a uniform reduction of par values) will move us to Zone I, where there is an excess supply of gold and an excess demand for dollars and sterling.

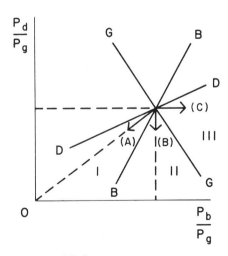

Figure 12-3

Devaluation in the sense (b) (a reduction in the par value of the dollar alone), will move us to Zone II, where there is an excess demand for dollars and an excess supply of gold and sterling.

Devaluation in the sense (c) (an appreciation of other currencies) will move us to Zone III, where there is an excess demand for gold dollars, and an excess supply of sterling and other currencies.

In all three cases the devaluation increases the excess demand for dollars, though by different amounts. In case (a) the pound is strengthened; in cases (b) and (c) it is weakened. In case (c) the excess demand for gold is increased while in cases (a) and (b) it is reduced. The choice of policies depends, therefore, on which of the different side effects are beneficial. We have to know the current state of basic forces in the market.

We have been speaking as if we are indeed talking about balance of payments and exchange rates, whereas initially we said that gold, dollars, and sterling were any three goods. There are many complications that need to be taken into account when making the transition from the model to the real world. One problem has to do with the multiplicity of currencies, and other markets; another problem concerns the balance of stocks in relation to flows. Actually, these problems are readily handled by general equilibrium methods, but the above analysis suffices for an introduction to the complications.

THE CURRENT POSITION

What, then, is the current state of disequilibrium in the world that suggests the need for any exchange rate changes?

The following basic disequilibrium patterns would probably be conceded by most observers of the international financial scene as of August 1968:

1. The French franc is overvalued with respect to the dollar.
2. The deutsche mark is undervalued with respect to the dollar. The Germans have recognized that they have to expand or else upvalue the mark; they have apparently chosen expansion. The French have said they would resist devaluation, but they have imposed controls of such a comprehensive scope that devaluation in the future may be necessary to remove them.
3. The U.K. position is less clear. The overhang of sterling liabilities is a mortgage on their resources, and many countries now want to leave the sterling area. U.K. vulnerability is reflected in their high interest rates, the discount on forward sterling, and the exceedingly weak reserve position. British labor, however, is not overvalued. Britain would be competitive if she could restore confidence in her capital position and could increase reserves at the going exchange rate.

4. The U.S. position is governed primarily by the *system itself*. For ten years we have heard much discussion of the U.S. balance of payments. The issue is sometimes posed in terms of whether the U.S. has a deficit or surplus, but these terms have rather little meaning for the U.S. Since the change in the system last March, the world has effectively moved onto a dollar standard. Access to U.S. gold stocks has been denied the private market, and it is effectively, if not formally, denied other central bankers. The primary question for the U.S., therefore, is whether U.S. financial policy is too expansionary or too restrictive, not whether there is a deficit or surplus in the U.S. balance of payments.

Looking at it in this way we have to ask whether the U.S. policy is excessively inflationary. That it was a few months ago was certain; but it is not so certain today.

Upvaluation of the mark and devaluation of the franc would be a step toward equilibrium; that much I believe is certain. Alternatively, deflation of the money stock in France and inflation of the money stock in Germany would help restore balance. But there is no compelling reason for a change in the price of the U.S. dollar in terms of foreign currencies. No country in the world wants to compete against a devalued dollar, with the possible exception of Germany.

We might briefly consider the theoretical consequences of an under-valued mark. Suppose we start out with an equilibrium, and then find that one of the currencies, the deutsche mark, becomes undervalued. We can test the implications of an undervaluation of the mark by considering the four-market system involving the gold prices of the dollar, pound, and mark. Our equations of equilibrium are

$$X_d\,(p_d, p_b, p_m) = 0, \tag{8}$$

$$X_g\,(p_d, p_b, p_m) = 0, \tag{9}$$

$$X_b\,(p_d, p_b, p_m) = 0, \tag{10}$$

$$X_m\,(p_d, p_b, p_m) = 0, \tag{11}$$

and Walras' Law:

$$p_d X_d + X_g + p_b X_b + p_m X_m \equiv 0, \tag{12}$$

where p_m is the gold price of the mark and X_m is the excess demand for marks. These equations determine the equilibrium values of the three prices.

Now, if we start with an equilibrium position and then differentiate the system with respect to p_m, it should be clear that some of the equations of equilibrium $(8-11)$ cannot be satisfied. In the context of the actual ex-ample, undervaluation of the mark, when other exchange rates are at their equilibrium values, implies an excess supply of dollars, pounds, and gold.

Diagrammatically, undervaluation of a currency other than the pound or the dollar means, in Figure 12-3, that *BB* is shifted to the left, *DD* is shifted down, and *GG* is shifted further from the origin; this leaves a triangular hole formed by the three quasi equilibria. As long as the gold price of the mark remains in disequilibrium, only two of the remaining three markets can be brought into balance.

The U.S. is, to be sure, committed to a social and economic policy that will lead to a higher price level than currently prevails over the next two or three years. It would not be possible to end the inflation quickly without bringing on a depression, and it would be disastrous for the U.S. to try to do so. But the case for devaluation has to rest on the need for a change in the system and not on the need to make any drastic correction for overvalued labor in the U.S.

In short, except for Germany and perhaps Holland, Switzerland, and Italy, no country would welcome an exchange rate change. It follows that if the U.S. were to lower its par value at the IMF, every other member of the fund would follow, with the possible exception of Germany, Holland, Switzerland, and perhaps Italy. But these countries already have the option of appreciation, and, so far, they have rejected it. Therefore, even those countries would probably not resist the de jure devaluation of their currencies. In short, there is simply no point to U.S. devaluation to change exchange rates because the devaluation would be followed by the rest of the world. To put it another way, the U.S. cannot devalue against other currencies unless the other countries will allow the U.S. to do so. There would be little or no point, therefore, to a devaluation of, say, 10 percent.

DEVALUATION AND THE SYSTEM AS A WHOLE

A far more respectable case can be made for devaluation to restore the gold exchange standard. The prerequisite for such a system to operate effectively is for gold to be worth more as money than as a commodity; there are three ways of bringing this about. One is to wait until South African supplies to the market are resumed. At such a time, gold would then be used as a money along the lines expressed by Gresham's Law.

A second method would be a new strategy of intervention in the gold market by the central banks. Collectively or individually, they could flood the market with existing gold stocks and determine whatever price they choose.

But the central bankers are today too nervous to follow such a bold policy; they have not yet lost their hunger for gold. At least they would not do so outside of an organization with wide participation. There is also the legal difficulty that the IMF is required to buy gold offered to it at the current price.

The third method is to raise the official price of gold. Provided it was a substantial increase so that speculation about a future increase is ruled out for some time, gold would flow out of hoards, and we would reestablish the gold exchange standard. Reserves would be centralized in the U.S. to an increasing extent, and the system would become similar to that which developed in the 1950s. How long it would last would depend on how high the price was raised.

DEFECTS OF THIS SOLUTION

The solution to halve the par value of all currencies (double the price of gold in terms of all currencies) cannot be rejected out of hand as a senseless solution to current problems. To solve problems of the system for even a decade and a half is not unattractive because it gives the monetary authorities fifteen more years in which to design a modern system. It is, indeed, the arrangement foreseen at Bretton Woods and embodied in the IMF Articles of Agreement. Despite some attractive features, revaluation has serious drawbacks:

1. Expectation of a second increase later on confers on gold a rate of return competitive with time deposits or other short term assets. Unless this expectation were dispelled there would be a relative shift in the demand for stocks of gold equal to the product of the interest rate implicit in the expectation of the higher price and the interest elasticity of demand for gold as a store of value. While this amount may be negligible for the first few years it would rapidly increase over time. The "gain" from the increase could well be dissipated within a few years.

For this reason alone an increase in the price of gold would be foolish unless it were associated with a resolve of the central banks to replace gold after the increase had taken place. As things presently stand, the SDRs are looked upon as a replacement for gold. The question then is whether these will become important enough in time to convince the market that the price of gold will not have to be raised again in the future.

Given success of the SDRs this argument against an increase in the price of gold falls to the ground. But the need for an increase has to rest also on the argument that there are no better ways of achieving the same objective.

2. A second objection to an increase in the price of gold is that it is potentially inflationary. It doubles the currency value of the gold component of reserves. Now a curious argument has got about that doubling the price is *not* inflationary because central banks do not have to use these reserves. The logic of the argument is extremely weak. Unless central banks are very short of reserves today, they will not hold a much larger amount. If central

banks were not responsive to reserve holdings, most of the arguments for and against liquidity would fall to the ground. What has the whole liquidity issue been about if it has not assumed some connection between actual reserves and the incentive to use these reserves?

Now, of course, central banks can write the new value of reserves down on their books in whatever form they want, and they can neutralize them in various ways. But will they? Will the Bundesbank act the same way with $12 billion of reserves as with $7 billion? Will Holland with $4 billion as with $2 billion? Will the U.S. with $24 billion? It is highly unlikely.

Let us grant temporarily, for the sake of argument, what seems quite absurd: that they would be willing to hold them. Even then an increase in the price of gold is inflationary; South African exports double in price, so that even if other prices stayed constant, some prices would rise in some countries.[5] At least the theory is clear. An increase in the price of gold is inflationary both because it increases world reserves and because it raises the value of South African exports.

The argument for raising the price of gold must then evaluate the need for an inflationary policy. In a state of world depression it would make sense. If the world moved into a state of serious depression, an increase in the price of gold might be the best way of increasing world reserves quickly, since we do not have, at the present time, any better way of managing a drastic increase in reserves.

But we are not in a state of depression today; the problem over the past three years has been excess demand and inflation. So on these grounds an argument for increasing the price of gold cannot be sustained.

Perhaps a reference to the diagram may help to make the point clear. If we double the prices of gold in terms of all currencies we move, in Figure 12-4, from the point Q to a point Q^* half-way along the ray OQ. Those who argue that an increase in the price of gold would not be inflationary are suggesting that there are no inflationary forces at the point Q^*. This is obviously untrue if the three schedules remain in their original positions.

But we do not want to accuse proponents of the view that an increase in the price of gold is not inflationary, of logical error; there is a set of premises that can rescue their argument. They would presumably say that the three schedules shift downward, presumably to intersect at the point Q^*. But what forces could produce a new position precisely at Q^*?

Q^* could remain an equilibrium only if the demand for gold simultaneously doubled with the increase in its price. It might be argued, for example, that the central banks want to double the ratio of gold backing

5. Of course South Africa could appreciate the rand, or impose deflationary export taxes.

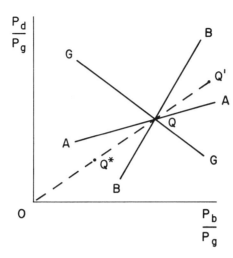

Figure 12-4

their monetary liabilities. This is probably not the case, but even if it were it would alter the flow supplies of gold and in this way affect the rate at which money supplies and prices were rising.[6]

> 3. The distribution effects of an increase in the price of gold are extremely arbitrary. a. South Africa's terms of trade would experience a great improvement; they would get a supplement to national income of at least $1 billion a year, worth $20 billion capitalized at five percent. b. French private hoards of gold are estimated at over 5,000 tons, so private gold hoarders in France would get a capital gain of over $5 billion. c. Owners of gold shares would benefit by fantastic amounts. d. Russia would reap substantial gains, and e. those central banks who converted dollars to gold would profit at the expense of those who kept dollars. Included among the latter countries are many countries who deliberately held on to dollars to help make the system work.

These redistributions of income and capital values may or may not be beneficial, but the countries are certainly not high on all lists of needy foreign aid recipients. Hardly anyone would deny that the list is capricious and arbitrary.

This does not mean that devaluation should be discarded on grounds of redistribution effects alone. If there were other compelling reasons for

6. The most consistent argument for increasing the price of gold is that advanced by Philip Cortney and the late Charles Rist, which, in terms of my Figure 12-4, would argue that inflation has pushed us to the disequilibrium point Q', and that failing an increase in the price of gold we are headed for a deflation to bring us back to equilibrium at Q.

raising the price of gold, it would be silly to give up this option solely because producers would gain from it. But none of the other arguments for it are convincing.

This leads us back to the original question: "should the U.S. devalue the dollar?" The question implies present circumstances.

The answer is, "No."

chapter 13

real gold, dollars, and paper gold

THE CAUSE OF CRISES

The system of periodic crises that began in October, 1960, and continued through 1968 is not over. We should anticipate further major disturbances in 1969 and the 1970s. Crises have become permanent stage props of the present system. An international crisis is one means by which a government can dramatize the need for an alteration in its policies and shift much of the blame for unpopular features of the new policy from the national government to the international community or to the dedicated little goblins lusting for gold.

It would be hard for a government to create a crisis out of thin air, but if the groundwork has been properly laid, a government can whip up a crisis in about two months. In the summer of 1968, for example, there was a steady outflow of capital from France. The signal for the crisis of November was the lifting of exchange controls in early September combined with the massive credit expansion inside France.

We are being partly facetious, of course, about the deliberate engineering of crises. It would be, perhaps, more judicious to say that the system as a whole has become less tolerant of mistakes in policy. The

Adapted from "Real Gold, Dollars, and Paper Gold," *American Economic Review* 59 (May 1969): 324–31.

power in the hands of private financiers has risen with the massive increase in international floating capital over the past few years. As long as the national reserves of each of the major countries were large relative to this private floating capital, a single country in isolation could withstand an attack. But the reserves of a large number of countries in the system are small in relation to the capital outflow pressure that can build up even in a few weeks. To keep control of the system now requires the collective reserves of the major countries. The central bankers who meet once a month in Basle have turned themselves into something like a floating first aid station, rushing monetary supplies to the next victim of speculative frenzy. The actual international reserves held by the major countries are small now, but the velocity of these reserves has been increased. We have fewer reserves in relation to the demands involved, more crises, and increased alertness in recognizing them and making them serve their social purpose.

It can be argued that the increasing frequency of crises is connected to the undervaluation of gold in the system. Suppose we start out with a system of currencies, goods, and gold and fix the price of gold in terms of currencies. Then allow a vast expansion of money, say, because of a war, which results in higher currency prices of all goods in the system except gold. Since gold is also a commodity, it will then be undervalued. Now take the most important of the currencies, the dollar; let all countries fix their exchange rates to the dollar, leaving the U.S. to keep the dollar convertible into gold at a given price. As long as the other central banks want to hold and accumulate both gold and dollars for use in their reserves, world inflation will have the effect of decreasing the residual supply available for central banks and thus drawing down or preventing an increase in the gold stocks of the U.S. more than would have been the case in the absence of world inflation. In a world where policymakers act on slogans rather than analysis, the problem will be misread as a balance of payments problem of the U.S. rather than as a problem of world inflation or the inadequacy of the reserve media.

To bring out the argument on a diagram let us restrict consideration to gold and three currencies: the dollar, the franc, and the mark. If the supply of currencies were in equilibrium at the existing price of gold, and if exchange rates were at their equilibrium level, we could find an equilibrium price for the mark and the franc in terms of the dollar at which there would be no excess demand for any of the currencies or gold; this point would be illustrated by Q in Figure 13-1 where all three curves intersect. But if currencies had been supplied to excess and world commodity prices had risen, there would be no single exchange rate for the mark relative to the dollar or the franc relative to the dollar that would clear all markets simultaneously; the original equilibrium would be a position of

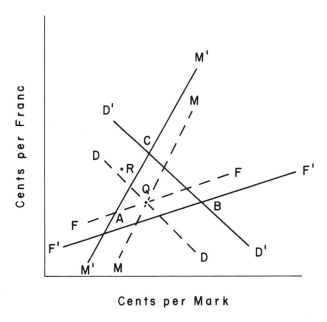

Cents per Mark

Figure 13-1   The dashed lines, *DD*, *MM*, and *FF*, intersecting at *Q* represent the initial equilibrium iso-balance-of-payments lines of the U.S., Germany, and France. Inflation with a fixed gold price has the effect of shifting these curves outward so that, at the original equilibrium *Q*, there would be an excess supply of all currencies and disappearance of gold into the private market. The system has no equilibrium until the real price of gold is raised either by price deflation or an increase in the currency price of gold; an alternative approach is to create a substitute, paper gold. The point *R* may be taken as the representative point in November, 1968.

excess demand for gold and excess supply of each of the other currencies. In such a case, exchange rates could be found that would equilibrate the French and German balances (point *A*); the French and American balance (point *B*) and the American and German balances (point *C*) but not all three balances simultaneously. The point *Q* would indicate deficits of all three countries and disappearance of monetary gold from central bank stocks. The point *R* would reflect the situation prevailing in November 1968, neglecting, of course, the fact that the price of gold in the free market is separated from the official price. During the November 1968 crisis the situation was at the point *R*, and the authorities had a hard time deciding which, if any, pseudoequilibrium to move toward.

The main point to be made with this diagram, however, is that crises are likely to result again and again when there is one price relationship that is not in equilibrium and all prices except that price can be changed. If gold is underpriced while the mark is undervalued and the franc over-valued relative to the dollar, exchange rate solutions can relieve the temporary pressure on one or another of the currencies until growth and an accumulation of demand for reserves create reserve scarcities for the next country. Faced with this situation relatively small disturbances can crack the system apart.

There are two basic paths out of the impasse. One is to raise the *real* price of gold; the other is to create paper gold. Now there are two ways of raising the real price of gold; the method chosen in 1930–34 was to deflate the world economy. This solution is rightly rejected universally by everyone. The other method is to raise the currency price of gold; opinion on the merits of this solution is divided. During the November, 1968, crisis a large number of economists favored a reduction in the mark price of gold, but there is a growing sentiment for a universal reduction in the par values of all currencies. This solution is not necessary and is far inferior to the managed use of paper gold in the system. Before developing this argument, however, it will be necessary to turn to the unique role played by the U.S. in the system and the malaise that is somewhat monotonously referred to as the U.S. balance of payments deficit.

THE U.S. DEFICIT

In order to focus attention on the failure of the world economy to attain balance in the context of growth, let us analyze it as we would a closed, integrated monetary system. Although this requires a leap of the imagination, it is fully justified in a world of fixed exchange rates and can indeed be derived from the aggregation of conditions of balance in a model in which an arbitrary number of national monetary systems are explicitly given full consideration. Monetary equilibrium in the system is dominated by the growth in the production of goods and services on the one hand and growth in the production of money on the other. Because it is a closed economy there is no net lending outside the system, so the excess demand for securities in it must be zero.

In Figure 13-2 real money balances are placed on the abscissa, and various rates of change are placed on the ordinate. The curve KK shows the relation between real money balances and the real rate of interest at which the world community is willing to hold the stock of capital. The curve MM gives the relation between real money balances and the money rate of interest at which the world community of central banks is satisfied with the real stock of reserves balances it actually has.

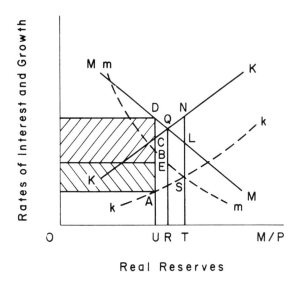

Figure 13-2 Rates of change are plotted on the ordinate and real reserves on the abscissa. *MM* plots the money-balance schedule; *KK*, the capital balance schedule. Rates of growth of money expansion are indicated by the vertical distance between *mm* and *MM*; rates of real growth by the vertical distance between *KK* and *kk*. In the nineteenth century the rate of real growth *NS* exceeded the rate of growth of gold production *LS*, and deflation at the *NL* ensued. Since 1958, however, rates of money growth exceeded rates of real growth *CA*, giving rise in rates of inflation *DC*. Gold production *DB* disappeared into private usage, and rate of monetary growth *DA* was provided almost entirely by the U.S., *DE* representing U.S. gold losses and *EA* the increase in U.S. dollar liabilities. The shaded areas give the absolute magnitude of the U.S. deficit.

If the world economy were not growing and no new money (e.g., gold) were being produced, equilibrium would settle at the point Q where MM and KK intersect. Real and money rates of interest would be equal (at the level QR) and the stock of real international money would be OR.

We must now take into account growth. At any moment of time the stock of nominal reserves balances is given, for the world as a whole, so that movements to the right and left on the ordinate imply lower and higher price levels, respectively. At each price level there will correspond a given rate of production of money and a given rate of production of goods. Draw *kk* to denote the given rate of goods production expressed as a proportion of the capital stock so that the vertical gap between *kk* and *KK* will indicate the percentage rate of goods production and therefore the commodity growth of the system. Similarly, draw *mm* so that the vertical gap between *MM* and *mm* indicates the rate of money production as a percentage of the money stock. Then equilibrium in the system will be established at the point where *kk* intersects *mm*; it is readily shown that *S* is the only position at which stocks and flows of goods and money are in equilibrium and where expected price changes are realized. At the equilibrium point *S* the desired and actual level of real money balances is *OT*; the real rate of interest is *TN*; the nominal rate of interest is *LT*; the rate of monetary expansion is *SL*; the rate of growth is *NS*; and the excess of the real rate of interest over the nominal rate of interest, *NL*, is the rate of deflation in the world economy. This configuration depicted at *S* might be taken to reflect the position of the world economy in the deflationary days of the gold standard between 1875 and 1895.

RESERVE CHANGES, 1958–68*

	ROW	U.S. Deficit
Gold	+10.5	− 9.9
F.E.	+ 8.3	− 7.2
Total	+18.8	−17.1

*International Financial Statistics (Dec., 1958–June, 1968). Measure of U.S. deficit excludes swap arrangements, IMF position and foreign exchange holdings; the latter amounted to $2.5 billion in June, 1968.

But we are interested in current events, not past history. From the end of 1958 to the middle of 1968 world monetary gold stocks did not increase; virtually all new gold production went into private hands. Monetary reserves of countries outside the U.S. did increase because countries acquired dollars and gold from the U.S. which they earned by generating balance of payments surpluses. The rest of the world (countries outside the U.S.) bought both dollars and gold from the U.S., who became over the period the sole supplier of reserves leaving aside IMF drawing rights.[1] Enough reserves were bought to finance a gently rising price level

1. The position is not altered even if IMF drawing rights are counted as part of liquidity because the important part of the increase in fund liquidity for the rest of the world was at the expense of the decrease in the fund position of the U.S. Normally the gold component of an increase in IMF quotas is financed by transferring U.S. gold to the gold component of the IMF, although a bookkeeping device was invented to disguise this fact in the most recent increase in quotas in 1966.

throughout the world. Thus the situation characterized by the dollar standard as it operated from 1958 to 1968 can be best portrayed by a lower supply of liquidity relative to capital, income, or trade, higher nominal interest rates, and perhaps real interest rates that were about the same as in the last part of the nineteenth century. In the diagram we can make the following average identifications for the period 1958–68:

$UD = i$, the nominal rate of interest
$UC = r$, the real rate of interest
$AC = \lambda$, the rate of growth
$AD = \rho$, the rate of monetary expansion in the rest of the world
$DC = \pi$, the rate of inflation

The distance DB represents both gold production and gold consumption (disappearance into the private market).

ED is the gold sales of the U.S. as a fraction of world reserves.

EA is the annual increase in dollars held by foreigners as a fraction of world reserves. The shaded areas represent the U.S. deficit, divided between its two components: gold losses and the increase in dollars held by foreigners.

Of course Figure 13-2 is an oversimplified presentation of the world system. What two dimensional representation could be otherwise? Its purpose is to dramatize certain relevant features of the world system and to emphasize how inadequately founded is that view of the world system which analyzes the U.S. on the same basis as any other country. The U.S. became the world supplier of reserves over the period 1958. It is not harmful, of course, to speak of a U.S. deficit any more than it would be harmful to say that the Federal Reserve System is in perpetual deficit because it pays out more dollars than it takes in. Words are harmless; it is the actions taken on misinterpretation of the meaning of concepts that do the damage.

The crucial points to be emphasized can now be summarized. Because the world economy is growing, countries collectively want to accumulate reserves. In order to accumulate reserves they try to run balance of payments surpluses, but they need an asset in which to hold their reserves. At present they can accumulate gold or dollars or some other national currency, but at the current price of gold there are no supplies of gold available to central banks. The U.S., however, has a special responsibility in the system. If other countries want gold they can take it out of the U.S. stock. Thus, the U.S. is the only source of reserves providing gold and dollars in the system. This is called the U.S. deficit.

The only way the deficit can be corrected is by making available to other central banks an asset that is not provided by the U.S. which has been up to now the only country willing to supply the reserves other countries want. No country other than the U.S. was willing or able to supply gold on demand for its currency; and no currency other than dollars was needed for exchange transactions. This is the reason why the U.S. has run a payments deficit from 1958–68, and why, in the absence of paper gold, it will continue to run deficits.

PAPER GOLD

We now turn to paper gold. The demand for additional dollar holdings will continue, but only in connection with another asset in the system. Real gold is no longer adequate to assure sufficient and sustained reserve growth. A paper gold solution is the only approach that can create the conditions for rational world monetary management, end the systematic crises, and end the U.S. balance of payments deficit.

There are several ways of creating paper gold. One is to create a right to draw on the IMF and give liabilities incurred a gold guarantee, as was done with the special drawing rights. This does not meet the basic world monetary problem; the instrument does nothing to solve the confidence problem; and the supply of SDRs that will be created will be inadequate. Over the next ten or fifteen years the world will need perhaps $50 to $80 billions of new reserves; my prediction is that the nations will not be willing to create even half of that amount of SDRs.

The best solution is to create paper gold by centralizing reserve assets. A number of plans for centralizing reserves have been discussed; most have parents in one of Keynes's or Triffin's plans. My own preference is to put all reserves into an international monetary pool (IMP) and use the certificates members get in exchange (intors) as world money. Since the March communique they could use a shadow price of gold as a new instrument. Suppose, for example, the countries contributed to the pool the following reserves: gold, one billion ounces; foreign exchange, $25 billion; other, $5 billion. The IMP would then have to decide how to value gold. Since the official market has been separated from the private market one could make a virtue of this separation and use the official price of gold as a regulator. Let us suppose that initially gold is valued at $35 an ounce. The initial balance sheet of the pool would be as follows:

THE IMP

Assets		Liabilities	
Gold	$35 b.	Intors	$65 b.
Other	$30 b.		
Total	$65 b.		$65 b.

Now suppose the members decided to increase the supply of intors by $3 billion a year for the next five years. They could acquire more gold, foreign exchange, or SDRs, creating intors in exchange. But this is no longer necessary. They have the other alternative of changing the value they place on the million ounces of gold. If they did not acquire any additional dollars or new physical gold stocks, the additional intors could be created through an increase of $3.00 an ounce in the gold price resulting in, at the end of the next year, the following balance sheet:

THE IMP

Assets		Liabilities	
Gold	$38 b.	Intors	$68 b.
Other	$30 b.		
Total	$68 b.		$68 b.

Eventually gold would be worth more as money than as a commodity and thus establish the two price system on a basis consistent with Gresham's Law. The free market price of gold could be dominated by the gold policy of the IMP. The major intervention currency, the U.S. dollar, would cease dealing in gold and deal only in intors to which the dollar would be fixed in value, and the exchange rate system would continue as before.

The essential point to notice, however, is that it is not tonnage that is required to make new international money. Paper gold is better than real gold.

CONCLUSION

We have now seen that increasing crises occur in the system because of the undervaluation of gold; that the elasticity of the gold exchange standard based on the U.S. balance of payments has enabled the system to operate successfully in the past decade; and that the use of paper gold is the only device on which a lasting world monetary system can be based.

chapter 14 international liquidity and inflation

The decision to create an international money (SDRs) brings to the forefront the question of our understanding of the principles on which the
introduction of the new money is to be regulated. Two questions in
particular stand out. First, should new international money be created
during a period of liquidity shortage? Second, what criteria can be used
to determine when there is a liquidity shortage?

Several years ago most officials would have said that new money
should be created during a period of liquidity shortage, and that inflation
could be used as a symptom of liquidity excess. Conventional reasoning
would argue that excess liquidity enables the authorities to follow more
expansive policies and to run higher balance of payments deficits or smaller
balance of payments surpluses while liquidity scarcity does the opposite.
In times of liquidity scarcity countries behave like deficit countries and
follow restrained monetary policies, whereas in times of liquidity surplus
countries act more like surplus countries and follow expansionary monetary
policies.[1] Given that the goal of international monetary policy is to
stabilize world prices and employment, therefore, liquidity should be
increased during liquidity shortage to inhibit deflationary tendencies and
decreased during liquidity surplus to restrain inflationary tendencies in
the world economy.

1. They may also follow more restrictive trade policies, but this would conflict with
the goal of optimum level of trade.

ADJUSTMENT AND LIQUIDITY

The problem, of course, is complicated by the interrelationship between adjustment problems and liquidity problems, which are connected by Cournot's Law. If world reserves are constant, the sum of balance of payments surpluses has to equal the sum of balance of payments deficits. If reserves are increasing there is an excess of surpluses; if they are decreasing there is an excess of deficits. Policy actions are dictated by the relation between desired and actual surpluses, which has to be inferred by the policies undertaken. When desired surpluses exceed actual surpluses countries tend to contract; in the opposite case they tend to expand. The question of the adequacy of liquidity therefore revolves around the question of whether that contraction or expansion is desirable or not.

To fix ideas, let us take as a goal a zero rate of world inflation. Let us divide the world, rather arbitrarily, into two parts. If both parts have excess deficits they will follow more contractionary policies; if they have excess surpluses they will follow more expansionary policies. At full employment the first case would be referred to as "liquidity shortage" in the sense of a policy imperative requiring more reserves; the second case would be a liquidity surplus and lead to a call for less reserves.

The problem is less clearcut when one part of the world has an excess surplus and the other part has an excess deficit. Then there is an adjustment problem. If the adjustment mechanism under fixed rates is working, one part will be expanding and the other part will be contracting. This situation is evidence of the adjustment mechanism at work. The problem, however, will generally be more complicated because the excess deficit may not equal the excess surplus so that fact, combined with differences in sizes of the two areas, can lead to worldwide inflationary or deflationary pressures.

To formalize the idea behind the generalizations in a diagram, let us divide the world into two parts, A and B (e.g., America and the rest of the world) and represent on the axes of a diagram (Figure 14-1) the money incomes of the two areas. Theory then supposes that there is a relation between needed liquidity and incomes in the two areas so that a liquidity line LL could be drawn with a negative slope indicating the locus of levels of incomes at which desired liquidity is equal to actual liquidity. For a given quantity of actual global liquidity there would be a liquidity surplus or shortage, depending on whether actual incomes were below and left of LL or above and right of LL.

There is a second question of the distribution of liquidity. There

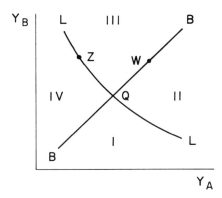

Figure 14-1

will generally exist a relation between money incomes in A and B at which the ex post balance of payments of each country is zero. Let us depict this relation by the line *BB*. Ordinarily *BB* will have a positive slope since a simultaneous improvement in the incomes of the two countries could preserve balance of payments equilibrium. Above and left of *BB* area *A* will have a surplus and area *B* a deficit; and similarly, below and right of *BB*, area *A* will have a deficit and *B* will have a surplus.

There are, then, two types of problems to consider. *Pure adjustment* problems prevail when the world economy is at a position on *LL* like the point *Z*. At this point global liquidity is correct, but A has a surplus and B has a deficit. At fixed exchange rates, A must expand and B must contract to achieve equilibrium at *Q*.[2]

Pure liquidity problems prevail when the world economy is at a position on *BB*, like the point *W*. At *W* there is a shortage of liquidity and, in the absence of additional liquidity creation, money incomes in both areas would have to decline. A point like *W* clearly represents the best case that could be made for an increase in liquidity since there is an appropriate increase in global liquidity that would shift *LL* upward and to the right so that it would pass through *W* and thus render unnecessary the deflationary policies needed to attain the point *Q*.

When the configuration of incomes in the two areas is not on either of the lines there are mixed liquidity and adjustment problems. Four situations may be distinguished as shown in the following self-explanatory table.

2. The relative degree of adjustment between the two economies will depend, of course, on their relative size. For a detailed discussion, see my *International Economics* (New York: Macmillan Co., 1968), chap. 13.

LIQUIDITY AND ADJUSTMENT PROBLEMS

Situation	Liquidity	Adjustment
I	surplus	deficit in A
II	shortage	deficit in A
III	shortage	deficit in B
IV	surplus	deficit in B

When expenditure is not on one of the curves global liquidity and adjustment policies will both be required.

THE JEURODOLLAR MARKET

The above analysis does not sufficiently recognize the subtlety of the interaction between money supplies, interest rates, inflation, velocity, wages, and the balance of payments; growth is not just a matter of time derivatives. Moreover, the "world economy" ignores the special character of a world economy that is, in an important sense, dominated by a large country, the U.S., and in which monetary events all over the world are connected to one another. Monetary policies in any of the major centers— New York, London, Chicago, Paris, Montreal, Zurich, Milan, San Francisco, Tokyo, Frankfort—affect the entire system. An open market sale of securities in London by the Bank of England tightens money all over the world just as do new sales by the Federal Reserve Bank of New York. The complexity of the links in the chain can obscure but not eliminate the connection. Tightness initiated by Europe raises Eurodollar interest rates, at least initially, draws funds out of the U.S. and Japan, and creates tightness in the New York and Tokyo markets; similarly, tightness initiated by the Federal Reserve System raises interest rates in New York, draws funds from the Jeurodollar market, and tightens interest rates there. If interest rates on assets denominated in national currencies are slow to respond, forward premia or discounts quickly emerge on the currency futures.

The U.S. currency occupies a special position in the system because it is the most important currency and the reference point of the system. Formally, of course, gold still occupies the position at the apex of the credit pyramid, serving the ceremonial function of restraining excessive dollar creations. Subject only to the weakly operative constraint of gold convertibility, the Federal Reserve calls the tune of world inflation.

Some of these institutional features can be brought explicitly into economic analysis. A more relevant analysis taking into account some of the special features of the world system can help to bring the constructions of theory that guide our thinking more closely into alignment with the data on which important policy decisions rest.

The purpose of the following sections of the chapter is, therefore, to clarify some of the relations between tight money, liquidity, inflation, growth, and the balance of payments in the context of the new international monetary system that has been evolving in recent years. The key element in the system is the role played by the U.S. balance of payments deficit as the pipeline feeding reserves to the rest of the world. In this system U.S. monetary policy plays a controlling role in influencing the world price level, subject to European acquiescence to a tacit agreement not to bring on dollar inconvertibility by running down U.S. gold reserves. This means that changes in U.S. monetary policy, conceived of as changes in the rate of U.S. monetary expansion, will affect interest rates, the foreign demand for dollar reserves, and the U.S. balance of payments deficit. The question then arises as to the balance of payments, interest rate, and price level effects in the markets we actually observe.

We shall see, after allowance is made for an initial adjustment of stocks of reserves, that an acceleration of U.S. monetary expansion

1. increases the dollar value of the balance of payments surpluses other countries want to generate;
2. increases the pace of world inflation and raises world interest rates on dollar loans;
3. can lead to a liquidity shortage at the time when excess liquidity appears greatest.

These conclusions have not always been fully realized by the monetary authorities, and yet they need to be taken into account in deciding on the quantity of SDRs needed.

EQUILIBRIUM IN THE ABSENCE OF INFLATION

In order to isolate the argument's essentials without reiterating propositions already known we shall use a stripped down model of the world economy. Assume it is divided into two parts: a reserve currency economy (country A) identified with the U.S., and the rest of the world (ROW). Assume also that confidence in fixed exchange rates is maintained throughout.

The stock of real international reserve balances (dollars) that ROW is willing to hold is taken to be a falling function, designated by ii in Figure 14-2, of the rate of interest on securities denominated in terms of

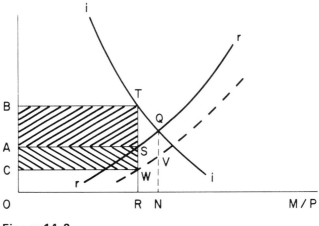

Figure 14-2

dollars,[3] this rate of interest being taken to represent the real opportunity cost of holding the dollars in liquid form when there is no inflation. For example, if the own interest rate on dollars were *RT*, the demand for real dollars (*M/P*) would be *OR* if there were no inflation at that interest rate.

Interest-bearing international reserves impose a cost on a country in the form of foregone interest income. Assume that ROW is a price taker on world commodity markets and that ROW has the additional choice of investing dollars in real assets. Assume, also, that the rate of return on real assets is a rising function of the quantity of real dollar balances that ROW holds.[4] Then we can use an *rr* schedule to depict the function connecting the own rate of interest on real goods in ROW to the quantity of real dollar reserves held. The monetary authorities will try to balance, at the margin, the social utility of holding dollars with the social utility of holding goods. This balancing process would equalize the rate of interest on dollar-denominated securities and the rate of return on real assets for the case in which there is no anticipated inflation or exchange rate changes.

If, for example, the dollar rate of interest were *RT* and the real rate of interest were *RS*, the quantity of real balances *OR* would only be the equilibrium level if inflation at the annual rate *ST* were anticipated. If inflation were not expected ROW would shift out of real assets into dollars until a level of real dollars, *ON*, were held such that the rates of interest on dollar securities and on real assets were both equal to *NQ*.

3. This model is almost the same as that used in chapter 13, although its interpretation is different.

4. Reserves increase the productivity of complementary resources because they enable a central bank to permit the community to adjust its inventories at a more optimal rate than is possible otherwise.

INFLATIONARY EXPECTATIONS

Now let us examine the implications for the willingness to hold dollars of an increase in the expected rate of inflation in A. Suppose the initial position is one of equilibrium at Q, but that this equilibrium is disturbed by expectations of inflation at the rate ST. How will ROW react to expected inflation? It will want to reduce its real reserves to OR, which becomes the equilibrium stock of real dollar balances.[5]

To summarize, then, the willingness to hold real dollar balances is *reduced* by expectations of inflation, and this fact alone induces ROW to shift out of dollars into goods. This change is a once-for-all adjustment of "velocity." But after this adjustment has been achieved there has to be taken into account the demand for the flow of additional dollars to replenish the steady depreciation of dollar reserves. Whereas initially ROW would want to maintain a zero balance of payments at the non-inflationary equilibrium Q, at the new inflationary equilibrium authorities in ROW will want to maintain a balance of payments surplus. The magnitude of this surplus will be equal to that additional quantity of dollars needed to compensate for the depreciation of existing reserve balances. In order to maintain the level of real money balances OR at a time when prices are rising at the rate ST, ROW must run a balance of payments surplus, expressed in current dollars, equal to the area $ABTS$.

The analogy to the well-known inflation tax argument is clear. By differentiating M/P with respect to time and setting the result equal to zero it can be seen that

$$\frac{d\frac{M}{P}}{dt} = \frac{P\frac{dM}{dt} - M\frac{dp}{dt}}{p^2} = 0, \tag{1}$$

whence

$$\frac{1}{p}\frac{dM}{dt} = \frac{M}{p}\frac{1}{p}\frac{dp}{dt}. \tag{2}$$

5. The reduction in real reserve balances held by ROW can be achieved in two ways: the immediate exchange of dollar reserves for goods before prices have risen; and the reduction in the real value of dollar reserves due to an increase in the price level. The latter involves a once-for-all tax on wealth on ROW residents equal to the reduction in real reserves, whereas the former possibility implies that ROW had been able to convert external reserves into goods *before* the initial adjustment of real cash balances to the lower level had taken place in the world as a whole. As is well known there is a cost imposed on dollar holders due to both a. the anticipation of inflation which requires an adjustment of income velocity; and b. the actual rate of inflation induced by monetary expansion itself. It is necessary to keep these two effects analytically separate, even if actual price changes in the real world are composed of both elements.

The dollar value of the balance of payments surplus of ROW is dM/dt, and its real value is $B/P = 1/P\ dM/dt$, the left hand side of equation (2). The right hand side is the product of two terms, M/P, the value of real dollar balances, which in the standard inflation-tax analogy represents the *base* of the tax, and $1/P\ dP/dt$, the rate of depreciation of the dollar balances, which in the inflation-tax analogy represents the *rate* of the tax.

Inflation in the reserve currency country thus imposes a tax on the rest of the world paid in the form of a transfer of real resources. To maintain the purchasing power of their reserves ROW must run a permanent balance of payments surplus with the reserve currency country, exchanging goods or claims in return for dollars that are yielding a negative nominal rate of return.

Thus we can see that while inflation in the reserve currency country causes a flight from dollars into goods in order to protect their country against the losses due to the increasing prices, it creates at the same time a desire for balance of payments surpluses in order to preserve the real value of dollar reserves, needed to compensate for their deteriorating real value due to secular inflation. Thus we may find all the symptoms of liquidity shortage indicated by attempts to achieve greater balance of payments surpluses through trade restrictions, tightening money market conditions, etc., in an environment of inflation. Inflation cannot therefore be taken as an unambiguous symptom of excess liquidity. Money can be tight in an inflationary environment.

A DIGRESSION ON GROWTH

We have up to now abstracted from considerations of growth. Strictly speaking, a consideration of growth is a digression from our central theme, yet neglect of it may be even more confusing than a cursory treatment of its place in the analysis. When an economy is expanding the authorities will generally want to increase *real* reserves to some extent. The extent of the increase will bear some relation to the rate of growth. The growth elasticity of demand for reserves will ordinarily be different, however, according to whether the growth originates in technological change, population increase, capital widening or deepening, improved resource allocation, or secular changes in the terms of trade. Because our interest is in the existence of a positive growth elasticity rather than in its size we will simply postulate, for present purposes, a given rate of increase in the demand for world reserves.

Let the distance QV be the rate of growth in new reserves desired so that, in the absence of inflationary expectations, ROW would want to run a balance of payments surplus equal to the product of QV and ON.

But let us proceed to our earlier case of inflationary expectations, now allowing for secular growth in real reserves. The latter will probably itself be a decreasing function of the inflation rate. If we use λ to represent the real rate of increase of reserves we have

$$\lambda = \frac{1}{\dfrac{M}{P}} \frac{d\dfrac{M}{P}}{dt} = \frac{1}{M} \frac{dM}{dt} - \frac{1}{P} \frac{dP}{dt} \, ,$$

so that the nominal rate of increase in reserves is

$$\frac{1}{M} \frac{dM}{dt} = \lambda + \frac{1}{P} \frac{dP}{dt} \, .$$

If, therefore, inflation at the rate ST is expected, the required rate of growth of nominal reserves will be TW, where SW is the value of λ corresponding to the inflation rate TS. The equilibrium real balance of payments surplus of ROW is therefore the total area $CBTW$, composed of two parts: $CASW$, which represents the real value of the additional reserves needed for growth; and $ABTS$ which is the real value of the "depreciation allowance" needed just to keep real reserves constant.

An illustrative example may help to provide a crude guide to the orders of magnitude involved. Suppose the countries of ROW wanted to increase *real* reserves at the rate of 3 percent a year. If inflation were going on at the rate of 5 percent a year, and total dollar and gold reserves of ROW were initially $60 billion, then ROW would want to run a collective balance of payments surplus of $4.8 billion, of which $1.8 billion would be needed to satisfy the real increase and $3.0 billion would be needed to compensate for the depreciation of existing balances. The $3.0 billion would be the yearly "tax" paid on dollar reserves, the transfer from residents in ROW to residents in the U.S.[6]

CONCLUSIONS

We have now seen that all the signs of an acute liquidity shortage can exist even though the world price level is increasing. This means that the need for liquidity cannot be judged solely on the basis of changes in the price level, since the creation of a liquidity shortage can bring in its

6. I am making no distinction here between citizens and residents. The $60 billion includes gold hoards, assumed to be fixed in price relative to the dollar. The analysis grossly exaggerates the "tax" because it does not allow for interest payments on dollar balances. The importance of seigniorage may not lie so much in the pecuniary loss as in the non-pecuniary effects associated with power and knowledge.

wake the restrictive commercial practices and tight money policies that are usually associated with monetary panics. It is, therefore, misleading to regard inflation as an indication of an excess of liquidity, since it is clearly compatible with the opposite.

Having said this, however, it is essential not to create the misleading impression that inflation does not give us valuable information about the need for liquidity. There is still a sense in which secular inflation is due to excessive liquidity. In the absence of a steady growth of reserves the inflation would not be sustainable in the context of an international system. If inflation ends, inflationary expectations are not viable in the long run. If reserve growth were suddenly ended monetary conditions would become tight, and expectations would be reversed. Residents in both A and ROW would adapt reserve holdings to the level appropriate to a non-inflationary path. In this sense the conventional conclusion, that excessive reserve growth can be blamed for inflation, is correct.

Assuming that it has been decided to slow down an inflation, a question arises as to the best means of accomplishing this end; this is a very complex operation. Monetary tightness will bring on a liquidity shortage. A liquidity shortage is the technique, in the international monetary sphere, for stopping inflation through monetary policy. The goal which international monetary reform was designed to *avoid* emerges as a prime instrument of policy. A liquidity shortage characterized by international tight money becomes a major object of policy.

If the system is inflating too rapidly and the Federal Reserve System (or, say, Germany) introduces monetary tightness, interest rates will initially rise until real expenditure has been restrained and expectations have been reversed. Subsequently, nominal interest rates will fall after the inflation premium has been taken out of dollar interest rates. The process of reversing expectations requires a liquidity shortage, i.e., international tight money. It would be a mistake, therefore, for the existence of liquidity shortage to be used as a signal for additional reserves.

What, then, is the purpose of additional international liquidity? New reserves redistribute the international *distribution* and *timing* of a world monetary squeeze. To achieve the same degree of international tightness the Federal Reserve, or the other initiators of the squeeze, would have to follow more restrictive policies than would otherwise be necessary. The correct time for the introduction of new liquidity is thus after the squeeze has been felt and expectations have been reversed, that is, when expansion is in order to prevent the squeeze from having recessionary carryover effects. In an integrated international monetary system the introduction of a new international monetary asset has, in principle, a greater impact on the *international distribution* of a liquidity shortage than on its magnitude. As long as the dollar remains the dominant currency the function of new liquidity is not to control inflation but to redistribute its burden.

chapter 15

the international distribution of money in a growing world economy

The purpose of this chapter is to analyze the conditions of world monetary equilibrium in a comprehensive bi-country framework that links inflation, interest rates, money stocks, rates of credit expansion, and the balance of payments in a growing world.

THE CONDITIONS OF MONETARY EQUILIBRIUM

The model we shall use for this purpose[1] requires balance in two markets: a market for claims against money and a market for capital against money. It assumes that in making the choice between holding money, claims, and capital the typical investor balances expected yields on each asset, where expectations are based on an extrapolation of current rates of change. Thus, if prices of commodities are rising at the rate π it is assumed that they will go on rising at that rate; and similarly for

1. A simple version of the model at the micronational level is given in my *International Economics* (New York: Macmillan Co., 1968), chap. 9; and in a somewhat different version at the macronational level, "Real Gold, Dollars and Paper Gold," *American Economic Review* 59 (May 1969): 324–31. Related theoretical work can be found in *Monetary Problems of the International Economy*, edited by Robert Mundell and Alexander Swoboda (Chicago: University of Chicago Press, 1969) and the contributions there of Grubel, Schmidt, Sjaastad and Johnson; also R. Komiya, "Economic Growth and the Balance of Payments: A Monetary Approach," *Journal of Political Economy* 77 (Jan.–Feb. 1969): 35–48; and a forthcoming paper by Arthur Laffer in the *American Economic Review*, including empirical tests.

changes in the prices of claims. This assumption, which would be fully justified only in consideration of an economy in growth-inflation equilibrium, enables us to isolate some important comparative dynamic properties of an international economic system and to develop a convenient representation of it in graphical form.

The line ii in Figure 15-1 refers to the money-claims market in which the nominal interest rate is taken to be a declining function of real money balances, plotted on the abscissa. At low interest rates the community is willing to hold the outstanding stock of securities only if the quantity of real money balances is high. When the rate of interest rises people shift out of money into claims, raising the price level and lowering the real value of money balances. We shall write this function as

$$i = i(m), \tag{1}$$

where $m = M/P$, the real value of money holdings, and i is the rate of interest paid on claims.

The rr schedule plots the relation between the real interest and the stock of real money balances at which the money-capital market is in equilibrium. It can be derived by making use of the extension of the diagram in the left-hand quadrant. The abscissa in this quadrant measures the quantity of capital, and the schedule KK indicates the stock of capital, a magnitude which is marching to the left over time under conditions of growth, but which at any instant can be regarded as given. The line m_0 identifies the schedule of the marginal product of capital corresponding to the quantity of real money balances m_0. This intersects the capital

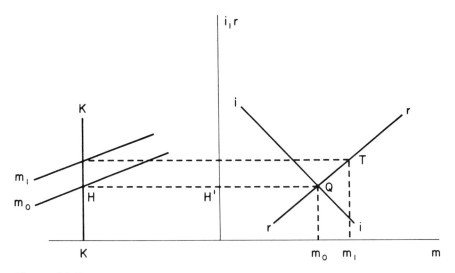

Figure 15-1

stock schedule KK at the point H and establishes the real rate of interest corresponding to the level of real money balances m_0. Thus Q is one point on the rr schedule.

Consider now an increase in the quantity of real money balances to, say, m_1. This raises the marginal product of capital and shifts the H line upwards, establishing a new point of equilibrium on the rr line at the point T. In a similar way all the points on rr can be established, and it is readily seen that this schedule must have a positive slope. We shall write this function in the form

$$r = r(m), \qquad (2)$$

where r is the real rate of interest.

The equilibrium interest rate and level of real balances is determined, in the absence of growth of capital or money, by the intersection of the two schedules, that is, at the point Q. The equilibrium condition is that $i = r$, so that

$$i\left(\frac{M}{P}\right) = r\left(\frac{M}{P}\right) \qquad (3)$$

determines the equilibrium level of real money balance, m_0. At levels of real money balances lower than m_0 the marginal product of real capital is lower than the marginal product of money, and asset holders would shift out of commodities into money, lowering the price level and raising the quantity of real money balances. To put the question differently, raising the rate of interest above r_0 would create an excess supply of money and capital and an excess demand for securities, inducing a fall in the rate of interest and a return to the equilibrium at Q. Thus Q is an equilibrium that is stable.

Now consider the effects of taking growth explicitly into account (Figure 15-2). Growth induces an increased desire for liquidity (hoarding) and thus an increase in spending less than the increase in real output. If we define the rate of growth in the demand for real money balances as a proportion of the capital stock, we can subtract it from the rr line to get $\lambda\lambda$. For simplicity of exposition we shall also identify this schedule with the rate of growth of output, an identification which is probably a valid approximation for certain types of output increases, but is precise only under specific assumptions about the income elasticity of demand for real money balances.[2]

2. Real money balances are a component of wealth and thus affect saving and the rate of interest [see my "Inflation and Real Interest," *Journal of Political Economy* 71 (June 1963): 280–83] while the rate of growth of output itself will be affected by the productivity of capital; on the basis of these considerations the hoarding could be made endogenous to the system. My concern in this chapter, however, is with the international aspects of a long term model, and it seemed appropriate to avoid overburdening the exposition with details I have worked out for publication elsewhere; hence my technique of treating growth exogenously.

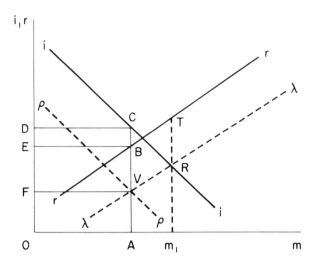

Figure 15-2   Inflationary Growth Equilibrium

When the economy is growing but the stock of money is constant, the equilibrium will be at R. The price level will be falling at a rate equal to the rate of growth, and the real rate of interest will be higher than the nominal rate of interest by the deflation rate RT. The condition of equilibrium is that

$$ i\left(\frac{M}{P}\right) - r\left(\frac{M}{P}\right) = \pi = -\lambda, $$

where π is the rate of inflation and λ is the given rate of growth. Holders of money and claims to nominal income streams will experience capital gains at a rate equal to the rate of inflation.

Now consider the effects of a positive rate of monetary expansion. This can be represented on the diagram by drawing a line $\rho\rho$ beneath ii such that the vertical distance between the two schedules represents the rate of monetary expansion. The equilibrium will then be determined at the point where $\rho\rho$ and $\lambda\lambda$ intersect. Thus, for the schedule drawn in the diagram, a new equilibrium is reached at V. The equilibrium is characterized by the following phenomena:

$r = OE$ = the real interest rate;
$i = OD$ = the money interest rate;
$\rho = FD$ = the rate of monetary expansion;
$\lambda = FE$ = the rate of growth;
$\pi = BC$ = the rate of inflation.

The equilibrium conditions are as follows:

$$i\left(\frac{M}{P}\right) - r\left(\frac{M}{P}\right) = \pi;$$

$$\rho = \pi + \lambda;$$

$$\lambda = \lambda_0;$$

$$\rho = \rho_0.$$

The comparative "statics" of the system are thus established. An increase in the rate of monetary expansion lowers the real interest rate, raises the money interest rate, and lowers the level of real money balances. This is readily seen by differentiating the above system and noting that $\partial i/\partial(M/P) < 0$ and $\partial r/\partial(M/P) > 0$.

MONETARY INTERACTION BETWEEN ECONOMIES

Let us now consider the situation that arises when it becomes necessary or useful to divide the world economy into two or more distinct parts. Assume that the two parts use the same money and freely trade in goods but do not lend to one another. What monetary relationships would we expect to emerge? Let us assume first that the money supply in the world as a whole is fixed.

The first relationship is that money will move from slow growing to fast growing regions. The inhabitants of the fast growing country will keep expenditure below output to generate a balance of payments surplus in order to finance money accumulation. This will exert deflationary pressure on the world as a whole. The effect, therefore, will be capital gains to the nongrowing region as the real value of their cash balances appreciates permitting them to export over time a fraction of their money stock to the other region. Equilibrium will be achieved when the world price level is declining at the rate sufficient to satisfy the desired increase in the real money stock in the growing country. The growing country finances its accumulations of new real money balances from two sources: a. imports of money from the other region and b. rising real value of hoards. The growing region's balance of trade surplus represents a transfer of resources to the nongrowing part analogous to the seigniorage gain when one country alone is the issuer of money.

The equilibrium is represented in Figure 15-3. Let us denote the two countries by A and B, the latter being the growing region. Equilibrium in the absence of growth would be established by the intersection of the rr and ii schedules in the two countries. Growth in B now involves a reduction in expenditure and releasing of goods for export (or reduction of imports) to finance money accumulation. Deflationary pressure in B then results in a flow of goods to A in return for more imports of money, while the loss of money from A and the hoarding of money in B combine to produce deflationary pressure in the world as a whole. The conditions of equilibrium require that deflation in both countries go on at the same rate because of the connected markets, means that the difference between real and nominal interest rates must be the same in both countries. A second condition is that the desired increase in real money balances in the growing country B be equal to the actual increase generated by the sum of the capital gains on their existing stock of real money balances and B's balance of trade surplus. The latter must be equal to the trade deficit of country A, which in turn has to equal the increase in the real value of existing money balances in A. Taken together, these conditions imply that

$$\frac{\lambda_b + \pi}{\pi} = -\frac{m_a}{m_b},$$

where the subscripts identify the countries. This means that the rate of world deflation due to growth in country B is

$$\pi = -\lambda_b \frac{m_b}{m_a + m_b},$$

that is, the rate of growth in B weighted by the size of B in relation to the world as a whole, the weights being the stocks of money. This result can easily be derived from the diagram since it implies that the two hatched areas are equal in area: they represent the real value of B's trade surplus and A's trade deficit.

It is a short step to take into account growth in country A. Growth in A creates more deflation in the world as a whole and diminishes A's deficit and B's surplus. When A and B grow at the same rate the deficit becomes zero, the appetite for real money balances in both countries being satisfied by the deflation in the world as a whole. This is readily seen from the generalization of the above formula:

$$\pi = -\frac{\lambda_a m_a + \lambda_b m_b}{m_a + m_b}.$$

MONETARY EXPANSION IN ONE COUNTRY

Let us now elaborate the model by allowing for monetary expansion. If, in Figure 15-3, country B had the right to issue money, the authorities could create it by purchasing domestic assets, fully satisfy the hoarding demand occasioned by growth, and eliminate the balance of payments

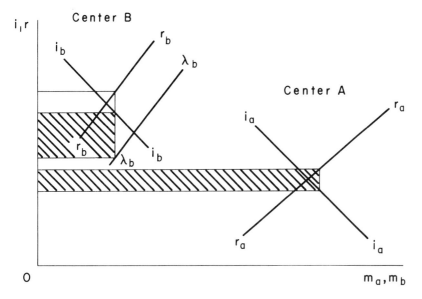

Figure 15-3   Exported Deflation from (b)

surplus. Insofar as the balance of payments surplus may be regarded as a tax, the monetary independence implied by the right to issue money would enable the residents of B to avoid paying the tax.

It will be somewhat more instructive, however, if we first analyze the equilibrium that results when country A has the sole right to issue money. Consider in Figure 15-4 a given rate of money expansion in A equal to the vertical distance between $\rho_a\rho_a$ and $i_a i_a$. If A were isolated this would result in inflation in A equal to the rate of monetary expansion and a transfer of resources from A residents to the government of A. But when country B is taken into account the rate of inflation in A is mitigated; the tax that A's government levied upon its citizens by the issuing of money will be paid partly by B.

The exact position of equilibrium will again depend on the relative sizes of the two countries. The conditions of equilibrium require that the rates of inflation in the two countries must be the same, and that A's deficit equal B's surplus. Thus the two hatched areas must be equal and

$$\rho m_a = \pi(m_a + m_b)$$

or

$$\frac{\pi}{\rho} = \frac{m_a}{m_a + m_b}.$$

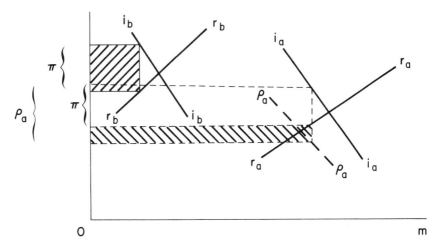

Figure 15-4   Exported Inflation from (a)

This ratio measures the percentage of the tax that is borne by the residents of A, whereas

$$m_b \pi = m_a(\rho_a - \pi)$$

measures the trade surplus of B and the trade deficit of A—the seigniorage tax accruing to A because of its right to issue "world" money.

Let us now analyze the more complete system that emerges when A is issuing money and both countries are growing. How will the new money be distributed between the two countries, and what balance of payments configuration will result?

The answers are provided in Figure 15-5. It will be convenient to identify five types of seigniorage arising from the monetary expansion in A. The total seigniorage is $\rho_a m_a$, which represents the purchasing power obtained by A's government when it issues money at the rate ρ_a, expressed as a fraction of money held in A. Internal seigniorage is the tax on A's residents, and external seigniorage is the tax on B's residents.

  I. πm_a = internal inflation seigniorage. This is due to the need of residents in A to rebuild cash balances eroded by price inflation.

 II. $\lambda_a m_a$ = internal growth seigniorage. This is due to the need of residents in A to add to real cash balances because of growth. External seigniorage is the tax on B's residents and is equal to A's balance of payments deficit.

III. $(\rho_a - \pi - \lambda_a)m_a$ = external seigniorage. This can be interpreted as the flow excess supply of money in A, her balance of payments "deficit."

IV. $\lambda_b m_b$ = external growth seigniorage. This arises from the desire of residents in B to acquire money to finance growth.

V. πm_b = external inflation seigniorage. This represents the real value of the desired increment in nominal money balances required to compensate for the capital losses suffered on existing balances.

Clearly, when A's ex ante deficit is equal to B's ex ante surplus

$$III = IV + V$$

and the system is in "equilibrium."

It will be convenient to have a symbolic characterization of some of these results. First, from the fact that total seigniorage

$$\rho_a m_a = I + II + III$$

we have

$$\rho_a m_a = \pi m_a + \lambda_a m_a + (\pi + \lambda_b) m_b,$$

so

$$\frac{m_a}{m_b} = \frac{\pi + \lambda_b}{\rho_a - \pi - \lambda_a}.$$

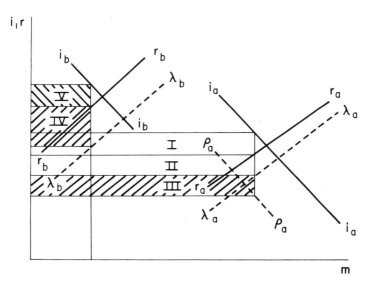

Figure 15-5   The Incidence of the Seigniorage
I.   A's internal inflation seigniorage
II. A's internal growth seigniorage
III. A's deficit
IV. A's external growth seigniorage
V.   A's external inflation seigniorage

$$III = IV + V$$

Now B's "desired surplus" is

$$(\pi + \lambda_b)m_b$$

and A's "desired deficit" is

$$(\rho_a - \pi - \lambda_a)m_a,$$

so that, when the two are in equilibrium the rate of inflation is

$$\pi = \frac{(\rho_a - \lambda_a)m_a - \lambda_b m_b}{m_a + m_b} = \frac{(\rho_a - \lambda_a)\dfrac{m_a}{m_b} - \lambda_b}{\dfrac{m_a}{m_b} + 1} = \frac{(\rho - \lambda_a)\sigma - \lambda_b}{\sigma + 1},$$

where σ is the ratio of money held in A to money held in B. The non-inflationary rate of monetary expansion in A is thus

$$\rho = \frac{\lambda_b}{\sigma} + \lambda_a$$

Thus when $\lambda_b = 0$, A's money supply must grow at a rate equal to the rate of growth of her economy if price stability is to be preserved. Other results of this kind are readily obtained from the formula.

"DEFENSIVE" MONETARY EXPANSION IN B

The monopolized right to issue money grants to A the possibility, not only the right, of determining the rate of expansion of the means of exchange and therefore, indirectly, the rate of change in the world price level; and also the means of taxing real resources from the rest of the world in addition to her own citizens: We shall refer to this right as the *issue privilege*. To offset it or to ameliorate its more outrageous effects, country B will create her own currency and confine her losses to the foreign exchange component of the banking assets which are the counterpart of the monetary liabilities. What effect will this have on the equilibrium?

It should be apparent that, for any given rate of monetary expansion in A, an increase in the rate of *credit* expansion in B is inflationary for the world as a whole. When there is an ex ante deficit in A the monetary authorities in B accumulate reserves. To resist undesired reserves they extend domestic credit and, in a sense, engage in competition for seigniorage that would otherwise accrue to A. The result is that the world price level as a whole rises at a more rapid rate than would otherwise occur. Suppose that, from a position of initial equilibrium, growth in B accelerates. This would ordinarily result in a surplus in B as residents hoard, and the result would be a deflation (or a slower rate of inflation) in the world as a whole as the ex ante surplus bids money away from A. But the demand-induced surplus in B can be prevented if B's authorities extend credit, assuming that B's money is convertible into A's money and is therefore a perfect substitute for it for internal transactions, and provide residents in B with the money they want through domestic banking operations. This prevents deflation or accelerates inflation, for if the government in B had not expanded, residents in B would have had to finance growth by sucking money away from the rest of the world.

We might also consider the effects of a credit expansion in B without any initiating increase in hoarding. The effect is to create an excess supply of money and an ex ante deficit in B so that its central bank will lose reserves. Unless the extension of credit in B is large, most of its effect will be taken up by a loss of reserves. But if B has initially very large reserves and can therefore afford a large extension of credit, the effects on the world money supply may be substantial, and there would result a significant effect on the world price level. For a given rate of monetary expansion in A, the potential increase in the world price level that could be induced by credit expansion in B depends on the ratio of the stock of reserves in B as a proportion of the world money supply. As this fraction increases the power of B to raise world prices is increased.

These results are useful first approximations, but they are not exact. To formulate more exact propositions it will be useful first to present the effects of credit expansion in B diagrammatically and then to develop the analysis in symbolic terms. It will simplify the diagrammatic exposition somewhat, without loss of essential generality, if we start off (Figure 15-6) with a situation in which the rate of credit expansion in B is zero and where the rate of monetary expansion in A is such as to ensure price stability in the world at large. A's rate of monetary expansion is AC, which exceeds A's rate of growth BC by enough (AB) to finance B's rate of growth DE without any changes in the price level.

Now suppose that from this position, where B is running a surplus to accumulate desired real balances, the central bank in B expands credit by the full amount of the surplus, i.e., at the rate ED. If A now reduced her rate of monetary expansion to BC, A's deficit and B's surplus would be corrected. But suppose instead that A maintains her rate of monetary expansion at the rate AC. Then the deficit in A is "unwanted" in B, and there is an excess supply of money equal to the area $FGDE = ABHJ$, and a corresponding excess demand for goods. The price level must therefore rise to absorb the excess money.

Where will the new equilibrium be? The answer is found by establishing that level of real balances in A at which two conditions are met. First, the excess of the money over the real rate of interest in A must

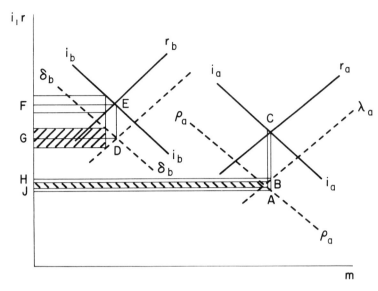

Figure 15-6   Defensive Measures in B

equal the excess in B. Second, the excess of A's rate of monetary expansion over the sum of her rate of growth and the rate of inflation multiplied by her stock of real money balances (A's ex ante deficit), must equal the excess of the sum of the inflation rate and B's growth rate over B's rate of credit expansion multiplied by the stock of real balances in B (B's ex ante surplus). The second condition means that the two hatched areas are equal.

We see, therefore, that B's attempt to eliminate her surplus is not wholly successful. The rate of credit creation DE causes inflation which increases the demand for additional money to compensate for the depreciation on existing balances.

To formulate the results exactly let us write the equilibrium conditions:

$$i_a(m_a) - r_a(m_a) = \pi = i_b(m_b) - r_b(m_b)$$

$$m_a(\rho_a - \lambda_a - \pi) = B = (\pi + \lambda_b - \delta_b)m_b$$

where B is the balance of payments deficit in A (surplus in B), and δ_b is the rate of credit expansion in B.[3] Now it is possible to see that when, initially, $\delta_b = 0$ and $\pi = 0$ the balance of payments deficit of A is

3. Differentiation of these equations with respect to δ_b yields

$$\frac{dm_a}{d\delta_b} = m_b \frac{(i_b' - r_b')}{\Delta} < 0,$$

$$\frac{dm_b}{d\delta_b} = m_b \frac{(i_a' - r_a')}{\Delta} < 0,$$

$$(\rho_a - \lambda_a)m_a = B = \lambda_b m_b.$$

When B now expands credit at the rate determined by the rate of growth of output, A's deficit becomes

$$(\rho_a - \lambda_a - \pi)m_a = B = (\pi)m_b,$$

which is still positive if B's credit expansion results in inflation, as indeed it must since it reduces the *excess* flow demand for money in A. To correct her surplus by her own actions alone B must expand credit at the rate

$$\delta_b = \lambda_b + \pi.$$

Now

$$\pi = (\rho_a - \lambda_a)\frac{m_a}{m_a + m_b} + (\delta_b - \lambda_b)\frac{m_b}{m_a + m_b},$$

or simply

$$\pi = \rho_a - \lambda_a.$$

Thus

$$\delta_b = \lambda_b + \rho_a - \lambda_a.$$

Country B's expansion rate must exceed her growth rate by the excess of A's rate of monetary expansion over A's growth rate. This is because the inflation itself induced by B's credit expansion increases the hoarding demand for money.

CONCLUSION

This chapter has presented an image of the world payments situation different from that found in the literature and currently used to interpret balance of payments statistics. For a given rate of credit creation in each of the countries the balance of payments is determined by the rates of growth of transactions and output.

$$\frac{d\pi}{d\delta_b} = \frac{(i_a' - r_a')(i_b' - r_b')}{\Delta} > 0,$$

$$\frac{dB}{d\delta_b} = \frac{m_b(\rho_a - \lambda_a - \pi) - m_a(i_a' - r_a')}{\Delta}(i_b' - r_b'),$$

where

$$\Delta = \begin{vmatrix} i_a' - r_a' & r_b' - i_b' & 0 \\ \rho_a - \lambda_a - \pi & \delta_b - \pi - \lambda_b & -m_a - m_b; \\ 0 & i_b' - r_b' & -1 \end{vmatrix}$$

the inequalities are based on the assumption that $\Delta > 0$.

In the real world, of course, rates of credit expansion are policy variables and will in most cases be positive functions of domestic growth rates. Domestic growth creates in the first instance a desire for increasing money which reduces expenditure below income, puts pressures on the credit markets, and generates a balance of payments surplus. The additional money will be automatically created as the central bank intervenes in the exchange market to prevent currency appreciation, thus creating domestic money at the same time that it adds to its holdings of foreign exchange reserves. To prevent unnecessary accumulations of reserves the central bank will purchase domestic assets, e.g., government bonds, and satisfy, by internal monetization, the growth-induced increases in desired cash. Different central banks, of course, will pursue different policies; some, for example, will try to maintain the same ratio of foreign reserves to central bank liabilities; others may vary the reserve ratio to keep domestic reserves a given fraction of imports. But in each case the autonomous variable in monetary policy is the rate of internal credit creation (the purchase of domestic assets), while the passive element is the rate of reserve increase. The public determines the quantity of money it wants to hold and the rate at which it is to be increased, while the central bank determines that part of it which will be backed by foreign reserves.

When we take into account interactions with the rest of the world, these propositions need to be adjusted. At the microeconomic level credit expansion has no effect on the money supply. But in the world as a whole a dollar's worth of money created anywhere in the system adds exactly that much money to the money supply of the system as a whole. At the microeconomic level the national communities determine the quantity of money they want. But at the macroeconomic level the nominal quantity of money is determined by the collective policies of the various central banks, while the world community as a whole determines its real value. If the collective money supply of the world economy is greater than the quantity desired, the world price level will rise until its real value has been adjusted to the level the community wants to hold.

This is not to say, of course, that the policies of various countries are symmetrical with respect to one another. Positions of dominance and subordination arise with respect to the different currencies. In the present configuration of the world economy the other nations keep their currencies convertible into the dollar, not the other way around. The U.S. monetary authorities are not constrained to govern their monetary policy by other than domestic considerations, since the only way the foreign central banks can avoid accumulating dollar holdings is by inflating themselves. The struggle on the part of the dominant country to acquire external inflation seigniorage at the expense of foreign countries and the resistance to paying the imposed tax on dollar balances can thus readily lead to a situation of competitive inflation.

chapter 16

european and american monetary policy

Important revisions in economic thinking are needed to understand the connections between growth, interest rates, and the balance of payments as they are determined under the modern gold standard. The theories of world monetary equilibrium of Hume, Ricardo, and Mill establish the nature of international general equilibrium for a static world economy, but need drastic adjustment to make them suitable for a growing world economy experiencing secular changes in the price level. An acceleration of monetary growth, for example, will initially lower interest rates, but insofar as the acceleration of monetary expansion leads to price increases that are anticipated, interest rates will eventually rise, altering the ratio of money to income and creating ambiguity with respect to the interpretation of the effect of monetary changes on the balance of payments. It is vital in all theories to specify the time period during which particular markets are allowed to adjust to equilibrium. Thus, distinctions can be made between theories based on hypothetical time periods during which

a. balances of payments are equilibrated,
b. capital stocks are relocated between countries, and
c. growth ceases.

Over the very long run it is necessary to allow for the rise and decline of different national currencies as international power relationships change.

CREDIT EXPANSION AND THE INTERNATIONAL DISTRIBUTION OF MONEY

In order to interpret the interaction between some of these variables and the instruments of international monetary policy it will be useful to construct a monetary model of the world economy, divided into two regions: America, and the rest of the world or "Europe."

In Figures 16-1a and 16-1b interest rates are plotted on the ordinate and real money supplies on the abscissa. $L_A L_A$ and $L_E L_E$ depict the liquidity preference schedules: the loci of interest rates and money supplies that indicate the willingness of each community to hold real money balances. These schedules can be symbolized by the equations $i = \phi(M_E)$ and $i = \psi(M_A)$ on the assumption that interest rates, after adjustment for exchange risk, are the same in each country.

In addition to the liquidity preference schedules we need equations specifying equilibrium in the world capital market. Assume that each country has a given labor force rooted to its respective region but that the capital stock, which is fixed in the short run for the world as a whole, is mobile between countries. The marginal efficiency of capital (*MEC*) is

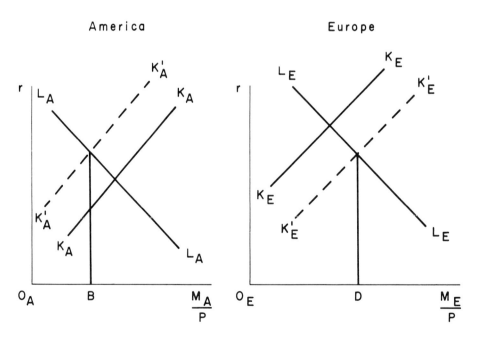

Figure 16-1a   Figure 16-1b

assumed to be an increasing function of real money balances and a decreasing function of the capital stock located in each region. Consider,
for example, the curve $K_A K_A$ in Figure 16-1a. This schedule indicates that
the marginal efficiency of capital (the real rate of interest) rises with the
level of real money balances for a certain quantity (K_A) of the world
capital stock located in America. If the amount K_A of capital is in America,
then $K - K_A$ of capital is located in Europe, where K is the world capital
stock, and this fixes the location of the corresponding capital equilibrium
schedule, $K_E K_E$, in Europe.

The implied distribution of the capital stock (K_A in America and
$K - K_A$ in Europe) is not an equilibrium quantity because the intersection
of $K_A K_A$ and $L_A L_A$ would result in a lower MEC in America than would
the corresponding intersection of $L_E L_E$ with $K_E K_E$ in Europe. Part of the
capital stock would accordingly move from America to Europe until the
MECs are equated. A migration of capital shifts $K_A K_A$ upward and to the
left and $K_E K_E$ downward and to the right. In the final equilibrium the two
schedules $K'_A K'_A$ and $K'_E K'_E$ establish the interest rate $BC = DF$ and the
level of real money balances, $O_A B$ in America and $O_E D$ in Europe.

In order to find the equilibrium of the system when the world economy
is growing and credit expansion in each of the regions is allowed for, it will
be convenient first to combine the two graphs. Adding $L_A L_A$ and $L_E L_E$
horizontally gives us (Figure 16-2) the global liquidity preference schedule,
LL; adding money supplies for corresponding capital schedules gives us the
global capital requirements schedule, KK. Let us assume, for simplicity,
that the income elasticity of the demand for money is unity. Then subtract
the rate of growth of the world economy from KK to get $\lambda\lambda$; this equals

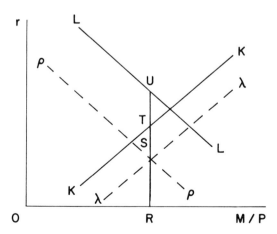

Figure 16-2

the real rate of increase in the demand for money. Now by an analogous procedure we can subtract the rate of growth in the supply of money from LL to get $\rho\rho$. The equilibrium of the system is determined at the point where the growth of the nominal supply of money is equal to the growth of the nominal demand for money. Taking into account the fact that the nominal demand for money is composed of two parts—a real increase and an increase needed to compensate for a depreciation of nominal balances due to inflation—it is readily established that the equilibrium of the system will be established at the intersection of the two schedules $\lambda\lambda$ and $\rho\rho$, since the rate of growth in the nominal demand for money will be the vertical difference between $\lambda\lambda$ and LL. Illustrative values for the variables at equilibrium of the G-10 (group of ten countries') economy in 1968 would be

$$M/P = OR = \$400 \text{ billion} \qquad \text{(money balances)};$$
$$i = RU = 7 \text{ percent} \qquad \text{(interest rates)};$$
$$r = TR = 4 \text{ percent} \qquad \text{(real interest rate)};$$
$$\pi = TU = 3 \text{ percent} \qquad \text{(rate of inflation)};$$
$$\rho = US = 6 \text{ percent} \qquad \text{(rate of monetary expansion)};$$
$$\lambda = TS = 3 \text{ percent} \qquad \text{(rate of growth)}.$$

Figure 16-2 enables us to find the equilibrium of the system under conditions of growth, but not the distribution of monetary growth between the two regions. Our major concern is the division of the money supply between the two regions and the balance of payments of the United States and Europe. To specify these variables the world economy must be broken into its component parts, as in Figures 16-3a and 16-3b. From the apparatus of Figure 16-2 we get the equilibrium interest rate and the position of the $K_A K_A$ and $K_E K_E$ schedules. The balance of payments of the two regions is then determined by the fact that any excess supply of money produced by one region must in equilibrium be equal to the excess demand for money produced in the other region. Since the rate of inflation is common to both regions, the balance of payments will be established at the point where the excess of the "equilibrium" rate of monetary expansion over the sum of the rate of growth and the rate of inflation in one region, weighted by the money supply of that region, plus the corresponding excess in the other region, is zero. The shaded areas in the left- and right-hand graphs represent the U.S. balance of payments deficit and the European balance of payments surplus. A representative value for this area is about \$4 billion, or 2 percent of the U.S. money supply.

Now consider the effects of an increase in credit creation in one of the regions, say the U.S. In Figure 16-3a this involves a downward movement in the curve $\delta_A \delta_A$ and a rearrangement of capital stocks between the countries. After an initial adjustment during which interest rates will fall,

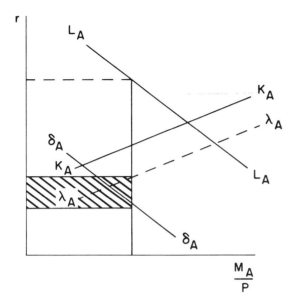

Figure 16-3a

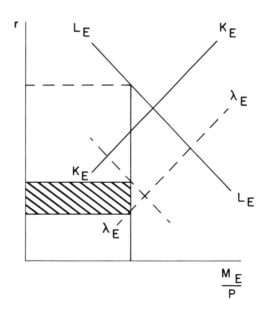

Figure 16-3b

the expected rate of inflation in the world will increase, lowering the real quantity of money demanded in both regions and raising the world price level. But after this adjustment process has been completed there will be an increased flow demand for money in both countries to compensate for the depreciation of real money balances. In the absence of any change in the rate of credit expansion in Europe, the U.S. balance of payments deficit will increase. An increase in credit expansion in the U.S. will therefore result in an increased monetary expansion in the U.S. that is less than the increased credit expansion, and there will be an increase in the rate of *monetary* expansion in Europe, arising from the balance of payments surplus, even though there is no change in the European rate of *credit* expansion.

We can see, therefore, that an increase in U.S. monetary expansion can lead to an increase in the U.S. balance of payments deficit. But consider now an increase in the growth rate in Europe which leads to an increase in the demand for money in Europe; this amounts to a downward shift in the schedule $\lambda_E \lambda_E$. In the absence of additional credit creation in Europe monetary tightness will induce a balance of payments surplus and an increase in the rate of monetary expansion and deflationary (or reduced inflationary) pressure in the world economy, again leading to an increased balance of payments deficit in the U.S.

MONETARY CONTROL OF THE SYSTEM

We have now seen how both an increase in the rate of credit expansion in the U.S. and an increase in the rate of change of the demand for money in Europe can worsen the U.S. balance of payments; these two possibilities are closely related to two theories of the U.S. deficit. One view of the deficit is that it arises from excess money creation in the U.S., which forces European central banks to accumulate dollars they must either hoard, giving a zero or low interest loan to the U.S., or get rid of by more expansive monetary policies, thus assuming an unduly large share of the burden of adjustment. This *supply theory of the deficit* suggests that the U.S. is to "blame" for its deficit, and U.S. action alone can correct it.

Another theory of the deficit is that it arises from the demand for reserve growth in the rest of the world. Foreign countries adjust their monetary policies to earn surpluses required for reserve growth. If the U.S. tightens money in an attempt to correct its deficit, the rest of the world will respond by tightening money policy in return in order to preserve the balance of payments surpluses needed for reserve growth. According to this *demand theory of the deficit*, the U.S. cannot correct its deficit until an alternative to the dollar or gold is found.

The Europeans have stressed the supply theory of the deficit, especially in the early 1960s, and urged the importance of early correction, while the Americans have stressed the demand theory, especially in the later 1960s, and the need for an early introduction of SDRs.

Our foregoing analysis shows, however, that it is unnecessary to resort to one-sided theories of the deficit or even to the concepts of disequilibrium they imply. The existence of the deficit is compatible with equilibrium between demand and supply over the past two decades, not only in the tautological sense in which demand and supply are always in equilibrium, but in the operational sense of equilibrium.

Consider again increased (desired) hoarding in Europe. In the absence of a corresponding acceleration of credit in Europe this will bring deflationary pressure in the world as a whole and a European surplus. However, the deflationary pressure may induce the U.S. monetary authorities to *accelerate* credit to maintain monetary growth in the U.S., or to *decelerate* it to prevent a worsening of the balance of payments. Similarly, an increase in U.S. credit expansion that worsens the U.S. deficit may induce additional or slower credit expansion in Europe as the authorities act, respectively, either to reduce their surpluses or slow the pace of inflation. The first European reaction would be equilibrating with respect to the balance of payments, but it would aggravate world inflation; whereas the second reaction would have the opposite effect. In none of these cases can it be said that the U.S. deficit is either demand-determined or supply-determined.

A central issue in the conduct of monetary relations between the two regions, therefore, is the type of reaction of one monetary authority to a change in policy in the other regions.

To investigate these interactions let us consider as two independent variables the rates of expansion of credit in the U.S. and Europe, δ_a and δ_e, plotted on the axes of Figure 16-4. The equilibrium relation between these variables and the rate of world inflation is

$$\pi = (\delta_a - \lambda_a)\sigma_a + (\delta_e - \lambda_e)(1 - \sigma_a),$$

where σ_a is the share of dollars in the world money stock. Price stability ($\pi = 0$) requires that changes in δ_a are offset by changes in δ_e. The line $\pi\pi$ depicts the values of δ_a and δ_e at which price stability can be maintained.

The second consideration is the U.S. balance of payments deficit. From Figures 16-3a and 16-3b it is readily seen that the deficit (B) is equal to $[\delta_a - (\lambda_a + \pi)]m_a = B = [(\lambda_e + \pi) - \delta_e]m_e$. There are variations in δ_a and δ_e that will preserve a given value of B; the zero balance of payments line is BB, and it has a positive slope. A simultaneous increase in both δ_a and δ_e will raise the rate of inflation, and both regions will have to par-

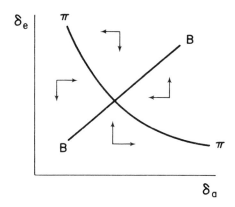

Figure 16-4

ticipate in the credit expansion producing it if a zero balance of payments is to be maintained.

Now consider a policy matrix based on the targets of balance of payments equilibrium and price stability.

Instrument/Target	Balance of Payments	Price Stability
δ_a	A	B
δ_e	C	D

Both countries could cooperate to achieve the same target following policies A and C (adjusting toward the BB line) or policies B and D (adjusting toward the $\pi\pi$ line). Or a division of functions based on A and D or B and C could be adopted. Slightly more complex possibilities with alternating roles could be adopted, with, for example, the surplus region assuming responsibility for adjustment when $\pi > 0$, and the deficit country when $\pi < 0$.

In fact, however, there is an asymmetry built into the system by virtue of the postwar position of the dollar as the settlement currency. The U.S. currency bloc encompasses a transactions area covering half the world, and its currency is an ultimate reserve. This fact imparts an asymmetry to the division of responsibility between Europe and America.

There are two aspects of the asymmetry, although they are closely related to one another. One shows up in the intervention system by which the U.S. fixes the gold price and other countries fix their dollar rates. Formally, the restraint on credit expansion in Europe is the requirement of convertibility of the national currency into the dollar, which implies equilibrium in the balance of payments subject to possibly variations in reserves. The formal constraint, on the other hand, is convertibility into gold. But convertibility of the dollar depends not just on the U.S. balance of payments, which is best defined as equal to the collective surpluses of Europe, but on the gold-dollar ratio of reserves abroad. However, U.S. policy cannot be dominated by the convertibility requirement, since any serious conflict between internal balance and gold convertibility of the dollar would probably be decided in favor of internal balance.

This leads up to the second aspect of the asymmetry, which stems from size. The U.S. constraint is not convertibility but the rate of inflation. In theory, therefore, the U.S. economy sets a given pace of inflation which, in view of the size of the U.S. transactions area, dominates rates of inflation throughout the world.

The pairing of instruments and targets is therefore suggested by the policy arrangement represented by B and C in the policy table: U.S. credit expansion is devoted to the world requirement of price stability, and European credit expansion is matched to the requirement of balance of payments equilibrium, as the arrows in Figure 16-4 indicate. The asymmetrical solution reflects the power position of the U.S. which can talk, in theory, with a single voice.

In the long run, however, retention of the monetary leadership in the U.S. will depend on the quality of U.S. performance, with erratic or antisocial behavior ultimately forcing Europe into a currency coalition. The greater the departure from acceptable norms the more likely is the emergence of monetary leadership in Europe.

chapter 17

seigniorage and the optimum world central bank

This chapter examines the optimum structure of a world central bank. The problem is to ascertain the relation between the interest rate on deposits, and the marginal product of capital, the division between earning and nonearning assets, and the method of introducing new reserves into the system. The chapter develops an explicit analysis of optimal proportions of "hard" and "soft" money in the international system, an idea which, in its theoretical developments, harkens back to Hume and perhaps Plato, but an understanding of which was the occasion of numerous monetary experiments in the Middle Ages.

In how many ways can a central bank be constructed? Probably an indefinite number. But how many *ideal* ways are there for a central bank to be constructed? Experience with optimum solutions in other branches of economic theory suggests that there may be only *one* way. But, if that is so, what *is* that one way?

This question may appear at first irrelevant and even irreverent in view of the number of alternative plans for reform which have been advanced. The question sounds rather ivory-towerish; that, however, can be rather a virtue than a defect. What unites economists is a common body of theory; in the field of central banking, theory seems far more difficult because every theory has an immediate application to policy, and we immediately encounter social or political obstacles. The best way for scientists to achieve unanimity, when that is desirable, is to study the theory of optimum structures. After the logic has been sorted out, compromise can come in the course of making concessions to practical reality.

MEANING OF OPTIMUM STRUCTURE

We shall take such a construction to mean specifications stating:

a. the interest rate to be paid on deposits
b. the interest rate to be earned on assets
c. the composition of assets
d. the method of introducing new reserves into the system.

The goal is to maximize real income, where the latter is taken to include the services of money looked at either as a productive factor or as a consumer service.

An ideal central bank would not, on the *highest level of economic abstraction*, hold real assets like gold if these assets had alternative uses, used up real resources to produce, and if cheaper substitutes were available. Given complete *trust* in a world authority and the willingness to relinquish sovereignty, the liabilities of the world authority would be accepted on fiat. But trust itself can be conceived of as an economic variable capable of economic analysis insofar as it depends on memory, inheritance and reserve ratios, and there is no reason why a system that takes into account incomplete trust has to be conceived of as a second best solution except insofar as we regard it a sensible use of scarce language to say that we live in a second best world. But it is necessary to keep the model as simple as possible. As Edgeworth says, we have to

"Deduct what is but vanity or dress
Or learning's luxury or idleness;
Mere tricks to show the stretch of human brain."

Let me use that imperative as an excuse for devising a model that ignores all those factors that seem to be irrelevant.

THE APPARATUS

Let us conceive first of a small country trading with the rest of the world at prices determined internationally. The inhabitants of the country can divide their wealth between international money and goods in any proportion the inhabitants choose. The simplest case, with which we shall

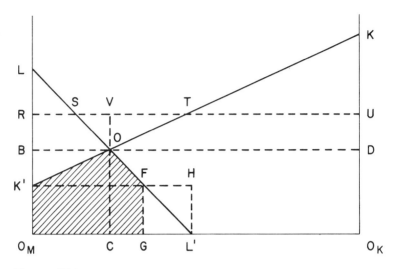

Figure 17-1

begin, is one in which the country's currency is either composed entirely of international reserves[1], which we shall refer to as gold, or else is backed 100 percent by foreign exchange or gold.[2]

The horizontal axis (Figure 17-1) portrays wealth, divided in some proportion between gold and goods; units are defined so that the gold price of goods is unity. The schedule LL' with origin at O_M describes the willingness of the inhabitants to hold the stock of currency at various levels of the rate of interest, given by the ordinate; the schedule KK' with origin at O_K similarly plots their willingness to hold goods at various rates of interest. It is assumed in the construction of LL' and KK' that the marginal productivities of gold and goods depend, respectively, only on gold and goods (a "separability" assumption), and that the areas under the curves—corresponding to any specific division of wealth between gold and goods—represent real national income, including the services of money.

In the absence of capital movements, equilibrium will settle at Q, where wealth ($O_M O_K$) is divided between currency and goods in the proportion $O_M C / C O_K$, and where the interest rate is CQ. That Q is the equilibrium point can be seen by considering an alternative interest rate such as $O_M R$ at which the community would want to hold RS of currency and TU of capital, so that the gap ST would imply an excess of the stock of securities supplied, a disequilibrium that would force the interest rate, in the absence of capital flows, to OB.

1. For example, Panama, Liberia, the Bahamas and some West African countries.

2. For example, some of the currency board systems of the British, French, or Portuguese colonies.

At Q real national income is maximized—given the assumed need to use international reserves as money—because the area under the two schedules, $O_M LQKO_K$, is at a maximum. We could allocate the national income as follows: $O_M BQC$ is the value of the services from money; $CQDO_K$, the value of the services from capital goods; and the triangles BLQ and KQD are rents to factors cooperating with money and goods, e.g., land or nontradable goods and labor, respectively.

There is no need at this stage of the analysis to take capital movements explicitly into account, but it is worth indicating that the conclusions would not be altered in any fundamental way by assuming capital mobility. Suppose that the interest rate abroad is higher than at home, say at $O_M R$, and that capital were free to move. Then SV of currency and VT of goods would be sent out to get ST of foreign securities. The area bounded by ST and the horizontal axis would represent income obtained from the net creditor position, and the increase in real national income (the gains from free capital flows) would be SQT. Analogous gains exist if the interest rate is lower than $O_M B$, making the country a net debtor rather than a net creditor.

CREDIT AS A SUBSTITUTE FOR MONEY

We are now ready to use the apparatus to discuss the difference between monies with and without real costs of acquisition. From the point of view of the country under consideration, the use of a foreign currency or gold as a domestic circulating medium is unnecessarily expensive. This was well known to the classical economists, of course; it was the whole point of Adam Smith's "highway in the sky." And John Stuart Mill wrote

> "The substitution, therefore, of paper for the precious metals, should always be carried as far as is consistent with safety; no greater amount of metallic currency being retained than is necessary to maintain, both in fact and in public belief, the convertibility of the paper."[3]

The extent of the gain from replacing gold with domestic paper is readily seen in Figure 17-1. Let us assume that virtually all of the gold could be replaced by domestic currency. This assumption is an exaggeration, of course, because it would not be possible to maintain convertibility without a gold reserve; it will, however, help us to draw sharp lines and will, in any case, be relaxed later.[4]

3. *Principles of Political Economy*, Bk. 3 (Ashley Edition, 1909). The theory was of course known long before, for example, by Hume and Smith.

4. G. S. Tolley has discussed some issues related to this chapter, in the context of the U.S. banking system, in his article, "Providing for Growth of the Money Supply," *Journal of Political Economy* 65 (Dec. 1957): 465–85.

Then $O_M C$ of gold could be exchanged for an equivalent amount of capital. But this would lower the domestic rate of interest to $O_M K'$, a rate at which the public would want to hold the larger quantity of money $K'F$. The gain in real income would be the shaded area $O_M K'QFG$. This gain is composed of two parts: the area $O_M K'QC$, which is the additional output accruing from a larger stock of real capital; and the area $CQFG$, which is the surplus attained from the fact that the addition to real capital has lowered the rate of interest and, hence, the cost of holding money, and has thus induced the public to hold a larger stock of money than was originally the case.

The means by which a country might effect such a replacement of foreign money by domestic money could involve ordinary open market operations. Purchasing domestic assets with newly created money would cause the exchange rate on new national money against gold to reach the gold export point; open market purchases would thus drive gold out of the country. The process can be continued, it is supposed, until almost all the gold in the country has been driven out.

It would, nevertheless, be wrong to suppose that we have now reached the optimum position—or even an equilibrium solution! In the process of acquiring domestic assets, the central bank also receives the income from these assets. If we suppose, for example, that in the process of encouraging gold to leave the country, the central bank acquires real assets and then relends them to the community at the going rate of interest, the central bank will receive interest from the community of an amount equal to rD, where r is the rate of interest and D is the total value of domestic assets.

In the absence of tax changes, and ignoring all the costs of creating paper money, the interest receipts will exert a deflationary effect on the economy. Perhaps it would be more correct to say that the steady decrease in the quantity of national money outstanding will generate a steady appreciation of the national money in terms of gold and real assets. In fact, if domestic assets replaced gold in the central bank's balance sheet, the new national money, M, is equal to D; thus $rM = rD$. But, since the interest payments represent a drain from the community to the central bank, the change in the money supply will be

$$\frac{dM}{dt} = -rM.$$

M will fall at a rate equal to the rate of interest on the bank's assets.

It is necessary to underline the significance of this fact. The natural process of replacing "barren" gold or foreign currency by domestic money involves a surplus for the central bank and, therefore, a deflationary solution. Prices would tend to fall at a rate equal to the reduction in the money supply. But, if national money appreciates in terms of goods, the cost of holding national money is lower by the rate of appreciation.

Indeed, in the pure case we have thus far developed in the diagram, the cost of holding domestic money becomes zero, and the public will now want to hold the larger amount $O_M L'$. By doing so, their real income will increase by the shaded triangle FGL'.

The complete replacement process thus yields a solution in which domestic money earns a real rate of return equal to the rate of interest on real capital. The public holds the optimum quantity of money, abstracting from the costs of creating paper or bank money. The solution is a deflationary one in which the own rate of interest on money is equal to the own rate of interest on other assets.

This solution is not the only one possible. An alternative solution is one in which the central bank pays interest on national money. Suppose, for example, the central bank uses all its interest receipts from domestic assets to pay interest on deposits; it turns back, in effect, its surplus to the public in a way in which the public regards it as a reward for holding deposits. Then, again, the optimal quantity of money, $O_M L'$, will be held.

It is important to realize that the interest rate paid on national money does not alter the *real* quantity of money that the public will hold in the case under consideration; it affects only the rate of inflation or deflation, and this offsets any effect on the real cost of holding money. If no interest is paid, national money will appreciate at a rate equal to the rate of interest, and the private marginal opportunity cost of holding money will be zero; if all the interest receipts are paid out as interest on money, the price level expressed in terms of national money will be constant, and the opportunity cost of holding money again will be zero. The cost of holding money in every case will be

$$C = r - i + \pi,$$

where i is the interest rate paid on money and π is the rate of inflation of prices. But the money supply will change according to the net outflow of money from the central bank. Thus,

$$-\left(\frac{dM}{dt}\right) = rM - iM.$$

Then, if $\pi = (1/M)(dM/dt)$, it follows that $C = 0$. The price level can change, but the real quantity of money remains at its optimum level.

THE COST OF HOLDING RESERVES

Thus far we have neglected the costs of producing national money. Money does cost resources—bank buildings, printing costs, and administration—to produce. But, at the present level of abstraction, we are more interested in a different form of cost: the cost of preserving confidence in the currency. Any central bank which expected to retain public confidence in the convertibility of its money at a fixed price without an external reserve would not last long. The size of the reserve that is necessary will depend partly upon the public's trust in the ability of the central bank to manage its affairs properly. External reserves represent an important part of the cost of producing domestic money.

New central banks usually have to start off with high reserve ratios. Trust is an increasing function of the reserve ratio, but it is also a function of time and the past history of the bank. A central bank that has a long record of success in maintaining parity with a minimum of noticeable crises will be able to get by on a relatively small reserve, as Britain managed to before 1914. In contrast, a central bank that manages its affairs in a chaotic way, going from one payments crisis to another, will be subject to withdrawals at the least disturbance, and will thus have to maintain a higher reserve even to stay afloat.

Our interest at the present time, however, is more in the implications of a given reserve ratio, rather than in establishing the factors determining what the level should be. Accordingly, let us restrict the analysis to the simple case where the central bank maintains a fixed reserve ratio.

Suppose that the central bank, instead of being able to replace the entire gold stock with national money, is committed to retain a reserve ratio of one-third in gold behind its liabilities. This is the reserve, we suppose, that is sufficient to maintain "in fact and in public belief" the convertibility of domestic paper. Where will the new equilibrium be and what will be the gains from this ratio as compared to a 100 percent reserve?

To answer this question we turn to Figure 17-2, which reproduces the essentials of Figure 17-1. Now draw LJ extended so that the horizontal distance between LJ and the vertical axis is one-third the corresponding distance of LL' from the vertical axis. This schedule represents the need for gold as backing against its domestic paper.

The intersection of the schedule LJ extended and KK' determines the solution that is obtained when two-thirds of the money supply, originally entirely gold, is replaced by domestic paper. The gains from the replacement of gold by paper are represented by the shaded area; this is, of course, smaller than the gains obtained in the preceding analysis. The envisaged mechanism under which the gains can be achieved is the same as before, except that the central bank now purchases assets up to the point where domestic assets are only two-thirds of its domestic liabilities.

Even so, we have not arrived at an equilibrium position. The same phenomenon discussed in the previous case arises; receipts accrue to the central bank, and this reduction in the public's money holdings exerts deflationary pressure. Either the central bank will have to dispose of its receipts, or the price level will have to fall—giving rise to a change in the

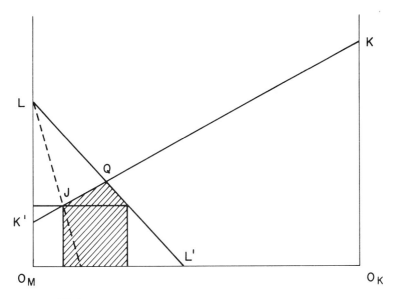

Figure 17-2

cost of holding money and an additional adjustment of real money balances.

Nor is the situation depicted in Figure 17-2 an optimum situation. The marginal utility of holding money is greater than its marginal social cost, as we shall see. Two forces are at work as additional money is held. On the one hand, additional money implies a larger stock of reserves held by the central bank, a cost factor. On the other hand, additional money held lowers its marginal utility. To find the final equilibrium, which is also the optimal solution, a more elaborate construction is needed.

OPTIMAL MONEY HOLDINGS AND
EXTERNAL RESERVES

The construction for the optimal solution is carried out in Figure 17-3, which retains the essentials of Figure 17-2. Extend KK' to the extended abscissa OO'. Draw $O'P$ extended with a slope such that NP is one-third of NW. The intersection of LJ extended and $O'P$ extended, at the point P, determines the optimum gold stock $O_M N$ and also the optimum money stock $O_M A$. At this position the rate of return on real capital is NW, and the cost of holding money is NP. The gains from the replacement of two-thirds of the gold stock, including the gains from the larger quantity of money held, are represented by the shaded area; this is necessarily larger than the shaded area depicted in Figure 17-2.

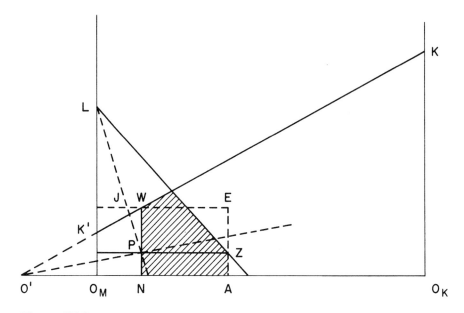

Figure 17-3

The public owns $O_K A$ of the capital stock outright and AN of the capital stock which it has borrowed from the central bank at the market rate of interest NW. But it receives interest on deposits, in the stable price level case, equal to the product $EZ \times O_M A$; this area is equal to the area $NWEA$, which is the total interest payment on loans.

The interest paid on money bears a precise relation to the ratio between earning assets and nonearning assets. Let B and M denote securities (bonds) and money, respectively, and r and i represent the rates of interest on them. Either competition or conditions of optimality would require—neglecting costs of providing, or additional advantages received from, banking services—that interest paid out equal interest taken in, so that

$$rB = iM \quad \text{or} \quad \alpha = 1 - \left(\frac{i}{r}\right),$$

where $\alpha = (M - B)/M$ is the fractional reserve ratio. The optimal (and the competitive) interest rate paid on money is therefore $i = (1 - \alpha)r$; it is the product of the interest rate on other assets and the bank's ratio of earning to nonearning assets.

That the situation depicted in Figure 17-3 is the optimum one is readily seen by noting that an extra unit of money created would increase real income by an amount equal to the marginal utility of money. For private holders the marginal utility of money is necessarily equal to the marginal cost of holding money, $C = r - i + \pi$. But to produce an extra unit of money requires additional reserves equal to α, the reserve ratio, and these reserves have to be acquired at the expense of the domestic capital stock. This means that they cost αr in terms of foregone output. Therefore, $C = \alpha r$.

Thus far we have been concerned solely with the arrangements that an individual bank and small central banks can or would make in devising an optimum structure in a world of many central banks. Before going on to consider the structure of a world bank, we should summarize some of the propositions we have already derived. A small central bank, in a static framework, should:

1. keep foreign reserves down to the minimum consistent with safety and confidence; in other words, it should economize on foreign reserves since these can be held only at the expense of domestic capital.

2. pay interest on domestic money, or allow appreciation of its currency at a rate equal to αr, which means—leaving aside other expenses of producing money—returning to the public the interest earned on the bank's fiduciary assets.

In making the transition to the world economy, however, we shall see that the gains which result from the attempt of each bank to economize on gold are not available to the world community looked at in the aggregate. There is a transition from microeconomic to macroeconomic principles in which the apparent gain to each bank, individually, disappears in collective action.

THE WORLD ECONOMY

We must now consider whether the propositions just reached also apply to the creation of a world central bank. When we move from consideration of a small economy trading with the rest of the world at given international prices to the world economy as a whole, it is necessary to take into account changes in the purchasing power of money over goods. The world economy is a closed economy, and we shall assume it to be integrated, in the sense of having a single interest rate.

Let us suppose that, initially, all countries are the same size, and then see the effects on the world economy of each national participant in it replacing a fraction of gold by domestic paper. Since we are, at this stage, abstracting from growth, we shall assume that there is a fixed stock of international money (gold).

A construction, similar to those developed earlier, can be used to depict the equilibrium in the world economy. In Figure 17-4, the horizontal axis represents the world stock of money and capital. The initial equilibrium at Q is determined by the intersection of the world demand schedules for capital and the *real* stock of gold. The schedules are given multiples of each of the national units. The difference between the initial situation in this diagram and the initial situation in those used earlier is that we must now deflate the stock of money by the price of goods, regarding LL' as a *real* demand for money. The gold price of goods, π, is now a variable instead of a constant.

For any given number of ounces of gold there will be a given equilibrium *value*. With gold as the sole domestic circulating medium in each country, the equilibrium is at Q. The world economy is a magnification of the national economies. But, if each country now tries to replace a portion of its gold stock, say one-third, by domestic paper, the quantity of money in the world would treble, and so would the money price of goods in terms of gold. This contrasts fundamentally with the microeconomic possibilities of a single economy that is small and acts in isolation. The real equilibrium is unchanged by the substitution of gold for goods, and there is no gain to the world economy from the replacement of gold by domestic paper. The real value of gold is reduced from BQ to BV, and the real value of domestic paper in circulation, in the world as a whole, is VQ. Some countries may gain individually by the substitution, depending on the time

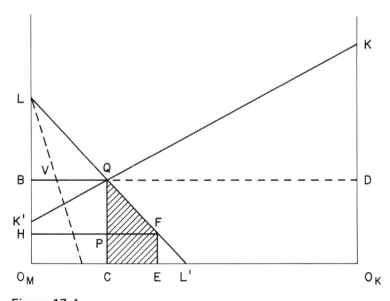

Figure 17-4

sequence by which the process is initiated, but they can only gain at the expense of other countries in the system.

Thus we see that, while the individual small country can gain by substituting domestic paper for international reserves when it acts alone, the world as a whole does not benefit by the process; and no individual country would benefit if the substitution occurred contemporaneously in all countries. Our first proposition does not hold in the context of the world community as a whole because the stock of capital goods in the world is fixed (at DQ) and the public can always determine the real value of the quantity of money in existence.

This is one of those important instances so familiar in economics in which the gains from individual action appear substantial, but disappear when all individuals act in a like manner. It is, of course, familiar in the field of monetary theory. Money is a component of private wealth, and it may even be interpreted as a part of public wealth—the patrimony of the country, a kind of public good. But if all individuals attempted to realize their money balances at the same time, that component of their wealth would be revealed as illusory.

It is important now, however, to prove two propositions: one is that ordinary competitive forces will result in a replacement of gold by paper money; the other is that, in so doing, the world approaches a more efficient state. Each nation will try to dispense with gold as long as gold is useful only as an international reserve. We have already seen the reason for this. Each country will serve its own interest without taking into account the needs of other countries. Suppose, for example, there is a community (it need not be a country) in which only external reserves like gold are used as money. It will become obvious to potential entrepreneurs that there is an externality that exists and can be exploited to make profits. The community needs gold only for external transactions; it can use paper for internal transactions. Provided the community is large enough, a bank will be formed to internalize the externality for the community; it will chase away unnecessary gold, replacing it with paper and getting capital in exchange. This we have already seen. Indeed, any number of banks will be formed, until the rate of return from an investment in banking is equal in all communities. The banks will buy up domestic assets and gold in the system and will hold the high-powered money reserve behind domestic paper. An international gold standard based on fractional banking will gradually emerge, created out of competitive forces. A pure gold specie standard is unstable, unless there are means of prohibiting the development of banks.

The process, however, also represents a move toward efficiency in the world as a whole. Suppose that confidence in exchange rates requires that each bank keep one-third gold as reserve behind its liabilities. The result would be, in the first instance, a tripling of the world price level. Historically, of course, joint stock banking did not require a tripling of prices because it took place over a substantial period of time, and the demand for money grew along with the money stock supplied. But there was a gain in efficiency in the process.

In the act of replacing gold by paper the banks will have acquired earning assets, and the profits on these assets will induce entry and competition until pure profits will have disappeared. The new equilibrium can take the form of appreciation of paper against gold or of interest paid on paper money. In either case, the public will now be induced to hold a larger quantity of money than before the replacement of gold, and that will imply a more efficient exploitation of the advantages of money.

In Figure 17-4, competition will induce a return on money paid either in the form of appreciation of the currency or interest on money deposits equal to QP, where QP is two-thirds of QC. Optimal money holdings will be HF, given the required reserve ratio, which has to be treated as a cost. The gain from the competitive process will be $QCEF$. The size of this zone of improvement should be compared with that available to an individual country acting in isolation. Real capital throughout the world is not created by the substitution process; one country can gain real capital only at the expense of other countries. The gain to world efficiency derives from the fact that competition forces banks to pay a return on money either in the form of interest, appreciation of capital value, or services.

Up until now we have assumed that gold has no alternative uses as a commodity. Starting from an initial position in which commercial banks or national central banks form to internalize for local communities the externalities associated with the possibility of economizing on gold, we have seen that bank notes or deposits, which serve the functions of money as well as gold, increase the nominal quantity of money in the world, and raise the world's price level. Bank notes can continue to be convertible into gold at a fixed rate, but the values of both gold and bank notes fall relative to the value of commodities.

But gold is, in the real world, as much a commodity as money. The falling exchange value of gold in relation to commodities would generate disappearance of gold from bank hoards into uses for industrial capital, jewelry, dentistry, and ornamentation. The social saving depicted in Figure 17-4, therefore, understates the gains that can be achieved by moving away from a pure gold specie standard. If gold could be absorbed into private industry at constant prices, the partial replacement of gold by paper in every country in the world would result in a gain analogous to that depicted in Figure 17-3, with the variables depicted on the abscissa applying to the world as a whole. Instead of a monetary expansion with inflation, the replacement process results in an increase in social capital and a pure gain.

GROWTH

We must now come to grips with the problem of optimal money holdings in a growing world economy. Suppose that a certain fraction of resources is devoted to the creation of new capital goods. Starting from an optimal level of world money holdings, we may ask how those optimal money holdings are altered by the fact of economic growth. Let us suppose also that the demand schedule for reserves is such that reserves must grow at the same rate as income; this would be a reasonable assumption if, for example, the growth is associated with population increases. With the central bank paying interest on money at a rate $i = \alpha r$, the demand for new money would create deflationary pressure, appreciation of money holdings, and an excessive quantity of money. Unless money is increased, the fact of growth would result in deflation; given an initial optimal holding of money balances, this would create a desire to hold money in excess of the optimal level.

To stabilize the world price level, the world central bank must generate a rate of monetary expansion equal to the rate of increase in output. One way to do this is to pay additional interest on paper money, but this would have the defect of inducing larger reserve holdings and excessive holding of reserves. The new money should instead be created in a way that does not alter the incentives for holding money.

The change in the money supply over time is determined by the operation of the central bank:

$$\frac{dM}{dt} = iM - rB + \frac{dB}{dt} + \frac{dG}{dt}, \tag{1}$$

where (dB/dt) and (dG/dt) represent the purchases of earning assets and gold, respectively, per unit of time. The private opportunity cost of holding money, C, is

$$C = r - i + \pi. \tag{2}$$

The social cost of creating real money balances is

$$C^* = \alpha r. \tag{3}$$

The optimal quantity of money implies that

$$i = r(1 - \alpha) + \pi. \tag{4}$$

But, as long as velocity is constant,

$$\frac{1}{M}\left(\frac{dM}{dt}\right) = \pi + \lambda. \tag{5}$$

Thus, inserting in (1) gives

$$\pi + \lambda = i - (1 - \alpha)r + \frac{1}{M}\left(\frac{dB}{dt} + \frac{dG}{dt}\right). \tag{6}$$

But, taking into account the optimality conditions (4), we have

$$\lambda = \frac{1}{M}\left(\frac{dB}{dt} + \frac{dG}{dt}\right) \tag{6}$$

$$= (1 - \alpha)\rho_b + \alpha\rho_g,$$

where ρ_b and ρ_g are, respectively, the rates of increase of earning and nonearning assets.

We may, therefore, conclude this section by summarizing the results thus far reached:

1. The optimal money holding is that which equates the private and social cost of holding money, which means that interest should be paid on money at the rate $i = (1 - \alpha)r + \pi$, where α is the gold backing behind money balances. The noninflationary solution means that gold certificates, or whatever the paper money created by the world bank is called, should pay interest equal to that fraction of market interest rates that earning assets bear to total assets of the world bank. If, for example, 100 percent gold backing were required behind gold certificates, no interest should be paid.

2. The fact of growth does not alter the basic interest rate optimality condition, except insofar as it affects the rate of inflation or deflation. Given the optimal level of reserves held in the absence of growth, growth would imply deflation, an appreciation of money balances, and an excessive monetary holding. The restoration of optimality conditions cannot be achieved merely by reducing the interest rate paid on money balances because that would generate a surplus for the bank and aggravate the deflation. The correct solution is for steady purchases of gold and earning assets at a rate equal to the growth rate, preserving the ratio of earning assets to nonearning assets. The result is a nondeflationary solution.

TRUST AS AN ECONOMIC VARIABLE

We are now ready to bring our analysis of an optimally constructed central bank to a close by relating it to institutions in the real world, even if only distantly. Let us suppose first that countries agreed to centralize their gold reserves and to use for international money instead the liabilities of a world central bank. Call them gold certificates. This change alone would involve no basic alteration in the actual operation of the system except that instead of gold, gold certificates would be held in central bank reserves. The objection to such a change is based on the war-chest argument and fear that any world central bank agency might in time of war freeze the assets of some of the belligerents. Insofar as the argument has any validity, it means that some countries might choose to retain an irreducible minimum of gold in their own stocks for the use of their generals. An alternative possibility would allow them to retain physical possession of the gold, "earmarking" it to the world bank, as Dr. E. M. Bernstein has suggested. In what follows I ignore any problems associated with this dimension of trust.

If gold is a useful commodity that can be turned into real capital without any drop in its price, an extreme assumption that somewhat exaggerates the social gain from replacing gold, the gold in the hands of the central bank could be exchanged for other assets and thus yield a social saving.[5] Costless money can do the job that was formerly done by a costly commodity; and it can also provide the means by which the central bank, through the acquisition of earning assets, can pay interest on gold certificates and encourage a larger holding of international reserves, adding to consumers' surplus obtained from holding precautionary reserve balances.

There is a case, therefore, that could be made for demonetizing gold completely and thus realizing the potential gain from replacing real gold with paper gold. All this, however, ignores psychological elements of trust and confidence that are based on historical considerations.

Trust has many dimensions: one involves confidence in policies (the *control* question); another involves the degree of concern over the value of assets. We shall be concerned here only with the second aspect, the value of assets, and ignore the problem of control.

Trust in the value of assets is a question of degree. A 100 percent reserve system is needed when confidence in the world money is totally lacking. No reserves are needed when confidence is entirely present. When countries make the institutional commitment to form a world central bank, they imply some degree of confidence and, therefore, some possibility of a fractional reserve system.

5. In calculating the value of the social saving one should include both consumer and producer users of gold. For example, the replacement of gold in central banks by gold certificates could, in principle, allow individual countries to dispense with prohibitions on the holding of gold by private citizens. Insofar as the elimination of these prohibitions would increase the demand for gold the central bank can exchange gold for other assets without lowering its price and thereby increase social welfare.

There are two possibilities, either of which could be adopted to develop a world money based on equal degrees of trust. One is to start off with a system relying only slightly on trust. This would be a system in which the central bank starts off with a high reserve ratio. From the initial position of 100 percent reserves, the world central bank could maintain, initially, a high reserve ratio, say one of 75 percent. In other words, it could replace 25 percent of its gold assets with earning assets, say dollars, and use the interest payments from the dollar assets to pay interest on gold certificates. In accordance with our optimality formula, the interest payment on world money should, in that instance, be one-quarter of the rate of interest on dollar assets, ignoring the expenses of running the bank.

As confidence and trust in the bank increases, the reserve ratio might be further lowered. Softening the hard-asset backing of the world money enables higher interest to be paid. The state of evolution of the world's monetary system would, therefore, be indicated by the ratio of gold reserves backing international money. Optimality, ignoring the cost of trust, would stipulate a complete fiduciary issue and interest on world precautionary money balances equal to the rate of interest, after allowance for risk, on other assets. But trust itself is an economic variable, and the cost of attaining it should not be excluded from explicit calculation.

On theoretical grounds, therefore, a full-fledged central bank, based on conservative principles (implying a low initial degree of trust), can be justified. Such a bank would centralize world gold holdings; but it would allow trust to evolve gradually, as the reserve ratio went down and the rate of interest on deposits went up.

A second possibility, based on a similar state of the world, is to use a very small quantity of international money with no reserve backing at all beyond the signature of "acceptability": rely on 100 percent trust in a small magnitude, rather than a small amount of trust in a large magnitude. By the nature of the concept, such an international asset would start off slowly and build its reputation up very gradually. But there is, unfortunately, no theoretical justification for such a system. If central banks are unrestricted in the use and composition of their reserves in a multiple asset system they will obey Gresham's Law and pay their debts with the softest assets; when all assets exchange for the same price the velocity of the cheapest asset becomes greatest.

It is for this reason that the second approach to a world money may be inferior to the first approach. The first approach is evolutionary rather than revolutionary and avoids the danger of swings in demand from one kind of international asset to another as expectations change.

index